The Autobiography of María Elena Moyano

D1524996

Florida A&M University, Tallahassee
Florida Atlantic University, Boca Raton
Florida Gulf Coast University, Ft. Myers
Florida International University, Miami
Florida State University, Tallahassee
University of Central Florida, Orlando
University of Florida, Gainesville
University of North Florida, Jacksonville
University of South Florida, Tampa
University of West Florida, Pensacola

The Autobiography of María Elena Moyano

The Life and Death of a Peruvian Activist

A Translation of *María Elena Moyano:*
  en busca de una esperanza

Edited and Annotated by Diana Miloslavich Tupac,
  The Flora Tristán Center for the Peruvian Woman (1993)

Translation, Prologue, and Afterword
  by Patricia S. Taylor Edmisten

University Press of Florida

GAINESVILLE · TALLAHASSEE · TAMPA · BOCA RATON

PENSACOLA · ORLANDO · MIAMI · JACKSONVILLE · FT. MYERS

LIBRARY OF CONGRESS CATALOGING-IN-PUBLICATION DATA
Moyano, María Elena, 1958–1992.
[María Elena Moyano. English]
The autobiography of María Elena Moyano: the life and death of a
Peruvian activist / edited and annotated by Diana Miloslavich Tupac,
translation, prologue, and afterword by Patricia S. Taylor Edmisten.
p. cm.
Translation of: María Elena Moyano.
Includes bibliographical references and index.
ISBN 0-8130-1810-2 (alk. paper); ISBN 0-8130-2746-2 (pbk.)
1. Villa El Salvador (Peru)—Social conditions. 2. Lima (Peru)—Social
conditions. 3. Moyano, María Elena, 1958–1992. 4. Women social
reformers—Peru—Villa El Salvador—Biography. 5. Feminists—
Peru—Villa El Salvador—Biography. I. Miloslavich Tupac, Diana.
HN350.V54 M6913   2000
303.48'4'092—dc21   00-026805
[B]

The University Press of Florida is the scholarly publishing agency for
the State University System of Florida, comprising Florida A&M
University, Florida Atlantic University, Florida Gulf Coast University,
Florida International University, Florida State University, University of
Central Florida, University of Florida, University of North Florida,
University of South Florida, and University of West Florida.

University Press of Florida
15 Northwest 15th Street
Gainesville, FL 32611-2079
http://www.upf.com

To the Memory of María Elena Moyano.

To the Women's Federation of Villa El Salvador

and to the feminists who continue to struggle for their utopias.

Contents

Editor's Preface

Shining Path guerrillas, Sendero Luminoso, assassinated María Elena Moyano and dynamited her body on February 15, 1992. They murdered her in the presence of her sons, Gustavo and David Pineki, while the family attended a community event sponsored by a Vaso de Leche [Glass of Milk] committee in Villa El Salvador [a large municipality near Lima]. Her assassination had an impact on all of Peru. A multitude attended her burial. Close to 300,000 persons accompanied the coffin in a monumental repudiation of the terror of the Shining Path. Why kill her? Assuredly, she represented hope to a country tired of violence and a danger to those who plotted terrorism.

With this book, I tried to recover the voice of María Elena Moyano a voice echoed by thousands of Peruvian women. The book consists of the reconstructed testimony of one of the best representatives of Peruvian womanhood of the last decade.

Her support for the development and centralization of the women's movement was significant. Her work in the community was innovative, spurring the formation of committees for the protection of the consumer. Her clear thinking and determination, in the face of violence, enabled us to look for peaceful alternatives to that violence. After being twice elected president of the Women's Federation of Villa El Salvador, she became deputy mayor of her district.

In this book, I tried to reconstruct María Elena Moyano's words— words that embrace a very significant and creative period for women in Peru. To retrieve her voice, to introduce her to those who did not know her, I gathered material from radio, television, newspapers, and magazine and book interviews that contained her statements. I organized the material by theme and date, designed the chapters, and added notes to give context to the information.

The book consists of two parts. The first part includes material related to her vision for Villa El Salvador, the Women's Federation, the Vaso de

Leche organization, the communal kitchens, local government, plans for pacification, and information about her encounters with terrorism.

The second part illustrates the strength of her love for her family, friends, and community as well as her tender nature. It contains her autobiography plus some notes she wrote just days before her death. I am including the autobiography exactly as she delivered it to me, because she wanted to have it published and because we had already been collaborating on this project. I have generally maintained the sequence of chapters and the format that we agreed on one evening in January 1992, a month before her death.

I could have gathered testimonials about her, but I wanted her words to speak for themselves. Those who assassinated her forgot that her example, her support for the Peruvian women's movement, and her tireless search for new political forms to help women achieve the power to transform the world continue to inspire.

Her murderers were mistaken if they thought they could make her disappear by dynamiting her body. She endures in the hearts and in the sands of Villa, where her ashes were scattered, as well as in the work of those who knew her. Beyond any doubt, María Elena Moyano compels us to continue the struggle.

Diana Miloslavich Tupac
Centro de la Mujer Peruana Flora Tristán
Lima, December 1992

Acknowledgments

To María Elena, for the friendship and strength she gave to me, converting my tears and pain into this book, despite her absence.

To the journalists—women and men—who interviewed her and made possible the reconstruction of her voice.

To Patricia Edmisten, for her interest in this book, and for her commitment to the women's cause in Peru.

To Gustavo Pineki, María Elena's companion, for his friendship and support.

To all of the *floras,* especially to Ingeborg Villena, with whom we continue to support the people's organizations.

To the recently founded María Elena Moyano Foundation and to Marta, María Elena's sister, its president.

To Nicolás y Felicita, my parents, who loved María Elena. To my uncle, Francisco Tupac.

To Nicolás, Milenka, and Carmen, my brother and sisters, who are always with me. To Rosina Valcarcel and Marta Meier for their solidarity. And to Luis M. Sirumbal.

Translator's Preface

María Elena Moyano and Diana Miloslavich Tupac, the Peruvian editor and compiler of this book, were good friends. The last days before her death, María Elena was staying in Diana's home. Before leaving for Villa El Salvador, on the day she would be assassinated, she and Diana ate breakfast together. Because they were close, this has not been an easy undertaking for Diana.

The personal dimensions of their friendship still rest in Diana's heart, perhaps to be included in a subsequent book, but the present work represents the highest tribute one friend can pay another. Diana has immortalized her friend; she has "reconstructed" her voice, enabling María Elena, despite death, to speak to her family, neighbors, friends, and politicians as well as to those who plot terror and death.

In October 1993, as a consultant for the United Nations, I visited the Flora Tristán Center for the Peruvian Woman. The center, located in Lima, was in transition. It faced new challenges and was emerging from a period in which its members, known affectionately as *floras,* or flowers, had been forced to lie low and to curtail their programs because of the fear generated by María Elena's assassination and the murders of other popular women leaders. I met Diana Miloslavich Tupac at the center and learned of her thoughtfully edited book about María Elena Moyano.

I had been a Peace Corps volunteer in Peru from 1962 to 1964 and was eager to return to the country that had played a significant role in shaping my personal and professional development. I am not a scholar of feminist theory, but of the sociological conditions that give rise to democracy and to educational practices.

The women's movement in Peru and throughout Latin America is inextricably related to the advancement of democracy. Those involved seek not only the full benefits of citizenship but also personal and professional relationships that correspond to democratic ideals.

As a twenty-three-year-old Peace Corps volunteer, I didn't think about women's suffering as a function of gender subordination. It's not that I was prepared to deny it; I just didn't think about it that way. I knew women's suffering was unjust, but I did not think in gender terms when I questioned why there were so many undernourished and sick women in Peru; why they gave birth to undernourished children; why their children died from diseases made unconquerable by malnutrition; why they had no medical care, or why so many of them died at an early age. I considered their plight to be part of the overall condition of poverty that beset the people with whom the volunteers worked, and, like so many others in the historical development of the women's movement, I believed the situation of women would improve if a more equitable distribution of land and wealth could be achieved.

When I returned to the United States, I was free to pursue my formal education, but it was my informal education, with the poor of Peru, that shaped me more than the years I spent in university classrooms. The women with whom I had worked could not pursue their educations; they had little time for anything beyond the acquisition and preparation of food and care of their families. They were too busy helping their families survive.

Patricia S. Taylor Edmisten

Chronology

1958   María Elena is born on November 23 in the Barranco district of Lima.

1970   Abimael Guzmán Reynoso founds Sendero Luminoso.

1974   María Elena graduates from secondary school.

1976   She becomes a teacher in a nonformal, experimental early childhood program.

1980   She marries Gustavo Pineki on March 28.

1983   She helps to found a mothers' club and becomes its director; she becomes secretary of the Popular Women's Federation of Villa El Salvador (FEPOMUVES).

1985–91   Three women activists are murdered.

1986   María Elena becomes president of FEPOMUVES.

1988   She is reelected to the presidency of FEPOMUVES.

1989   She is elected deputy mayor of Villa El Salvador.

1990   Peruvian president Alberto Fujimori institutes economic austerity programs.

1991   Sendero Luminoso plants a bomb in Vaso de Leche distribution center on September 9 and blames María Elena Moyano. Women's groups hold mass demonstration and march against hunger and terror. *La República*, one of Peru's leading newspapers, names María Elena "personality of the year."

1992   In defiance of Sendero Luminoso, María Elena leads a march against violence on February 14. Sendero Luminoso assassinates María Elena on February 15. Guzmán is captured on September 12.

Prologue

Women in Peru

A History of Struggle and Courage

The 1990s bore witness to a vast movement of Peruvian women who were organizing to improve conditions for themselves and their families. They challenged local and state governments to deal with survival issues, they stood up for their rights and championed peaceful negotiation over armed confrontation, and they used their solidarity to bring about social justice. The search for solutions to survival problems, engaged in by individuals or groups of women, primarily from the poorest economic class, is frequently referred to as popular feminism by Latin American scholars.

In a complementary way, some Latin American feminists were asking the fundamental question: why have women been subordinate to men? They rejected the hierarchical power structure that placed them in a culturally and economically subordinate role. To avoid hierarchical traps, they developed their own democratic organizations and networks. In the process, they discovered how deeply ingrained the tendency to resort to authority was and to look to it for guidance and decisions. They also learned that it takes time and effort to achieve consensus, and it takes active participation by all members.

Early History of the Women's Movement in Peru

The women's movement in Peru, like that in the rest of the South American continent, can be traced back to the nineteenth century, to the "watersheds" of the movement—the term used by Maritza Villavicencio, a Peruvian researcher. These watersheds represent the diverse "spaces" that women have occupied. The flow from these watersheds has been discontinuous and has coincided with the specific personal and professional arenas that women inhabit.[1]

In the 1860s, Latin American women gathered in private homes for "literary socials," where they read and discussed the ideas of the day, expressed in literature, poetry, philosophy, and politics. Later, the "generation of the nineties" worked to achieve technical education for poor women and "home economics" for women of the higher classes, all within the context of educational rights for women, a subversive activity during that epoch.[2]

Peruvian women who identified themselves as feminists emerged at the end of the nineteenth century and were joined by working women in the early years of the twentieth century. In 1917, a group of male workers was massacred north of Lima. In response, a group of working women assembled to honor the men. Newly developing bonds among women resulted in the formation of the Committee for a Lower Cost of Living. This assembly, composed of women from many walks of life, represented the first Peruvian feminist mobilization of the twentieth century, according to Virginia Vargas, who, in 1979, founded the Flora Tristán Center for the Peruvian Woman.[3]

In 1924, Magda Portal, a Peruvian poet living in exile in Mexico, became one of the founders of the Alianza Popular Revolucionaria Americana, known to this day as APRA. The American Popular Revolutionary Alliance rose in response to imperialist, clerical, and feudal land traditions in Peru. Its platform called for the incorporation of Peru's Indians into political life. Portal characterized APRA's program as "anti-imperialist, for the unity of the peoples of America, and for the realization of social justice." However, Portal, like so many contemporary women, believed that feminism pitted women against men. She declared that "the aprista woman [a member of APRA], who professes our ideology, does not want to conquer her rights through an open fight against men, as 'feminists' do, but to collaborate with him as her companion."[4]

In 1933, Peruvian women received the right to vote in municipal elections, but the constitution still referred to citizens as property-owning men. Although Portal did not have property in mind when she expressed her reservations about women and the vote, she shared the predominant male view that women's choices must be carefully guided because "the cultural level of the Peruvian woman, her prejudices, her unquestioning dependence on masculine influence, and often, on clerical influence, makes the female vote a measure to better support conservative ideas than revolutionary ones. . . . Consequently, the woman aprista—the woman worker, the woman of conscience—believes that the female vote must be qualified."[5]

Portal assumed that social and class revolution would bring justice to women because it righted the wrongs inflicted on poor and indigenous peoples, and because it determined its own future, independent of foreign influences. She was a brave woman, frequently imprisoned for her political stands, but she disliked feminists because of their upper-class origins.[6]

In 1945, Portal organized an eight-day women's convention in Lima that attracted married women, including Indian women, their husbands, and teachers. The delegates referred to their organizational units as "*comandos femininos.*"[7] Portal had earlier organized a women's section of APRA but soon found, despite the success of the women's convention, that the women's platform, originally accepted by APRA, was soon set aside by the party. She perceived this as a betrayal of APRA's goals and an indication of overall compromises that separated the party from its original ideals, which called for "the realization of a new democracy with liberty and social justice."[8]

Eventually, Portal left APRA, having realized that her vision for the party—that social and class reform would naturally include women as it bettered society—was not the vision held by APRA men. Francesca Miller summarized her plight: "Despite her loyalty, her lifelong service to aprista ideals, her imprisonment and exile, she was discounted by the male leadership because she was a woman."[9]

APRA's Second Party Congress met in Lima in 1948. Portal expressed her disillusionment: "Women are not active members of the Party, they are only *compañeras,* because they do not have the quality of citizenship. And what does it signify that we have fought during twenty long years, when after all the victories were exclusively for men?"[10] When Portal pressed her agenda, she was told there was nothing left to say. She walked out of the congress and was subsequently divested of her secretary-generalship and demoted to second undersecretary.

Twenty years earlier, in 1928, the Inter-American Commission of Women (IACW) was launched as a result of women's lobbying efforts at the 1928 International Conference of American States in Havana. Its charge was to investigate the "legal status of women in the twenty-one member states." It was "the first governmental organization in the world to be founded for the express purpose of working for the rights of women."[11]

In 1938, IACW met in Lima. The Mexican delegation proposed the Declaration in Favor of Women's Rights, a move to support the ratification of an article to the 1917 Mexican constitution redefining "citizen" to include both men and women.[12] Groups allied with IACW's goal of organizing women in "defense of democracy" emerged throughout the Americas.[13]

Acción Femenina Peruana (Peruvian Feminist Action) included teachers and nurses and working-class members of trade unions. In 1942, the branch in Arequipa, Peru's second largest city, declared that its overall theme would be the pursuit of "justice for women," counting the improvement of women's wages among its objectives.[14]

Military dictatorships emerged in the post–World War II period in many Latin American countries. Peru was no exception. There were acceptable activities for women, but they did not include militant demands for rights. According to Miller, "By the late 1950s the fiery zeal of the early feminists was no longer apparent: The 'first wave' of feminism in Latin America was at ebb tide. The older generation of feminists was dying or dead; the causes around which they had rallied were no longer in the political foreground."[15]

Special Plight of Andean Women

Until recently, Andean women have been outside of the women's movement, an ironic reality, given the long history of abuses they have suffered. According to Sonia Montecino, Andean women are a human metaphor for a geographical and cultural conquest. The Spanish violently penetrated them, took them as war booty, awarded them as prizes, and sold them as slaves. Indian women and Spanish men engendered a new race and a new culture—the mestizo—outside of their respective social and religious boundaries.

Even in cases where Spanish men loved Indian women, they could not marry, and so their offspring had no inheritance of land or wealth. In most instances, the fathers were not even physically present for their children.

This situation did not cause the children to forget their fathers. Just the opposite. Many preferred to be white, or criollo, to speak the language of the whites, to wear their clothes. They disdained the native Indian blood passed on to them by their mothers, and a race-conscious society justified that disdain. The women who birthed a nation of new people became reminders of the original coupling—something to be forgotten.[16]

Base Christian Communities and Popular Feminism

Base Christian communities sprang up throughout Latin America after the 1962–65 Second Vatican Council, called by Pope Paul VI to revitalize the Church and to evaluate its place in the modern world. These communities adopted a religious philosophy that proclaimed an "option for the poor," the revolutionary idea that the poor did not have to wait until they reached heaven to enjoy the kingdom of God—that they had a right to participate in that kingdom on Earth. Care of the soul was important, but so was care of the body and its needs. This attitude, interpreted as a theology of liberation by many clergy, declared the equality and dignity of all human beings and encouraged the poor to study the Scriptures to discover their preferred place.

Social activism among women flourished as part of this movement. They organized mothers' clubs in their parishes to ease the effects of economic crisis and resulting social disorder. In their own clubs, women were free to share their burdens, identify with each other's problems, and ask questions about health, child care, or relationships with their spouses. They could even feed their families by sharing food and cooking responsibilities. Individual women realized their problems were not unique, and this realization prompted them to question their patriarchal society, including the role of the Church in their lives. They could express their anger and talk about personal issues such as the need for birth control and freedom from domestic violence. Many of these clubs have since become independent of the Church.

The Academic Stream of the Women's Movement

Emerging in the seventies, the academic stream of the women's movement was composed of women from the middle class, mostly intellectuals, many of whom had political experience. These women expected and demanded full citizenship. Some of them had earlier been drawn to the study of Marxism in their quest for an understanding of the subordination-of-women phenomenon, but they did not find answers there. "The movement did not mature," according to Virginia Vargas, "until it gave up the idea that Marxism held all of the answers and until it rejected Marxists as spokespersons for the movement."[17]

The women who considered themselves to be both feminists and activists on behalf of social justice for the poor formed consciousness-raising groups and organized themselves to act upon their concerns. Several women's institutions emerged during this period, the most significant Peruvian organizations being the Flora Tristán Center for the Peruvian Woman and the Manuela Ramos Movement, the latter name signifying "everywoman."[18] Other Peruvian feminist organizations included Acción para la Liberación de la Mujer Peruana (Action for the Liberation of Peruvian Women, or ALIMUPER), Mujeres en Lucha (Women in Struggle), and the Frente de Mujeres Socialista (Women's Socialist Front), all of which elected representatives to a coordinating committee.[19]

Human Rights

During the seventies, too, many Latin American women became active in human rights movements in response to the abuses of military dictatorships. Their demands focused not on gender but on the authoritarian, brutal, and capricious activities of men who sequestered, tortured, "disappeared," and executed women and men who purportedly differed with their regimes. Nevertheless, the visibility of these women, as in the case of the Mothers of the Plaza de Mayo in Chile, put male officials on notice that these women would testify to the abuses their loved ones suffered, and that they would press their quiet and dignified demands until the country and the world heard them. And the world saw and heard these courageous women! They never let us forget the faces and names of their loved ones by standing up to the grotesqueries of government minions who pretended to preserve democracy while subverting it.

There was a dovetailing of the goals of the women who struggled for human rights in the seventies and those who called themselves feminists. This fusion was evident at the 1975 International Women's Year Meeting, sponsored by the United Nations and held in Mexico City, and it was evident throughout the next ten years, which had been declared the International Decade of Women by the United Nations. Women demanded an end to systematic rape, beatings, and other abominations endured by imprisoned women living under dictatorships and an end to the brutal treatment and casual disregard of the human rights of women who live in war zones. Elizabeth Jelin summarized the link between a woman's autonomy over her body and human rights: "Ultimately, the guarantee that the body of a woman will not be subject to actions without her consent and willful cooperation implies the recognition of *basic human rights:* this can be interpreted as part of the right to life, to freedom; as the proscription of slavery, bondage, torture and cruelty" (Universal Declaration of Human Rights, articles 3, 4, and 5).[20]

The international meeting also opened the eyes of feminists from the North, especially of those from Europe, who previously had little understanding of the extremely oppressive conditions under which many of their southern sisters from the popular classes were living. European and North American women's ideas about the process of liberation could not obtain in the South, but solidarity and cooperation emerged between these women from different continents.[21]

Migration, Population Growth, and the Feminization of Poverty

By the seventies, the gradual shift from agrarian to industrialized societies in Latin America had led to migration and cultural upheaval. Infant mortality had decreased, and people lived longer, causing unprecedented population growth. More people needed work. Economic growth continued until 1975 in some countries and until the early eighties in others, resulting in the reorientation of governmental roles and policies toward further economic and industrial development. These changes caused a massive swelling of the population in urban areas and an increased demand for government to provide health, education, and housing assistance. Governments became more complex, and many new public workers were added to governmental payrolls. The expectations of the people rose, and governments could no longer deliver. Economic growth did not lead to wealth sharing but to greater enrichment of those who were already well-off and to the growing ranks of the poor.[22]

Many Latin American countries are considered to be dependent capitalist. That is, they are dependent upon the demand that wealthy capitalist countries have for their exports. Food that could be raised for internal consumption, for example, is raised by the poor to feed the wealthy in their own country or for export, in return for a little cash. And, as these countries moved toward greater industrialization, without the training required for employment, women became marginalized in jobs that brought little remuneration. Hours were long, conditions might have been dreadful, but other poor women were always ready to take the job of one who complained. Many women became domestic servants within the homes of the wealthy, where they could be subjected to authoritarian relationships with their employers. Other women tried to earn a little cash by becoming *ambulantes,* street vendors.

International Assistance and the Burden of the Poor

To get financial assistance from donor governments or international development agencies, to continue payments on their debts, or to provide basic services, bankrupt countries were forced to remove subsidies from such staples as bread, milk, cooking oil, and sugar. They raised the cost of public transportation, upon which the poor depended, and they were forced to lessen allocations for the health, nutrition, and education programs that most benefit the poor. (In the nineties, for example, although the Peruvian economy appeared to be improving, according to a *Wall Street Journal* report that Peru achieved "the world's highest growth rate in 1994, with an expansion of 12 percent,"[23] governmental economic adjustments had devastating effects on the poor, the majority of whom were women and children.) The adjustments likewise undermined the small middle class, causing entrepreneurs to lose markets and to scramble for other sources of income.

Women who left their Andean villages to escape rural violence or to improve their families' economic situations were also affected. They traded their agrarian way of life, where they had some independence and control, for a culture in which the subservient treatment of people of indigenous origins prevailed. They had to learn Spanish, because the majority spoke Quechua or Aymara, and they had to adjust to a cash economy instead of to a system that relied on the reciprocal offering of goods and services.

The Women's Movement in the Eighties

In the eighties, women from the popular classes were developing an awareness of what Hannah Arendt called their "right to have rights."[24] More poor women joined cooperative organizations to soften the hardships caused by the economic crisis. They collaborated with other women to share the economic and labor costs of feeding their families. New types of social movements were developing throughout Latin America with goals that were closely linked to daily life. Women found bountiful opportunities to participate and many paths toward increasing self-esteem and personal empowerment. They became more aware of the failings of the state and of its power to change the civic and social conditions in which they lived, and they wanted a greater role in decisions affecting themselves and their families.

Academic feminists had another agenda in the eighties. They were demanding sovereignty over their bodies. A woman's body, without her consent, should be considered a no-man's-land. Furthermore, academic feminists viewed these rights as human rights that, in a democracy, should be respected.[25] Self-determination and autonomy over their own bodies were the foundation for the acquisition of other rights.

Democracy is born in the hearts, and only then can it be applied to government institutions. Marta Lamas expressed it well when she described the women's movement as "a subterranean river."[26] This river, unnoticed from above, fed many thirsty women through its streams, creeks, and branches.

Sendero Luminoso (The Shining Path) and the Peruvian Military

While many women worked for a peaceful and democratic revolution, other malignant forces determined that Peru was ripe for a violent revolution. Peru was and remains one of the poorest countries in Latin America. Nearly 40 percent of Peruvians are malnourished. Two-thirds of Lima's six million residents live in poor barrios, or shantytowns. The newer ones are referred to as *pueblos jóvenes,* young towns, because they were recently established by persons migrating from the sierra to urban areas.

In existence since 1970, Sendero Luminoso, the Shining Path, did not launch its terrorist activities until 1980. Abimael Guzmán Reynoso, Sendero's leader, became known as the "Fourth Sword of Communism." He followed the flaming swords of Marx, Lenin, and Mao. Guzmán had been a philosophy professor at the University of San Cristóbol de Huamanga in Ayacucho, a relatively isolated and poor district capital. His followers incorporated the most brutal methods of the Chinese cultural revolution to destroy Peruvian institutions and topple its government.

According to Carlos Iván Degregori, Sendero saw Peru as a semifeudal country, and any change of government would not change that status. A revolution required "an ideological rigidity unprecedented in Peruvian political history. To resist the powerful currents sweeping the left nationally and internationally, Sendero turned to a fundamentalism that maximized and lionized violence."[27]

Sendero viewed social organizations, staffed by individuals who wanted to help the poor, as useless. These groups were special targets because they attempted to mend existing political and social structures. Sendero wanted a country with no government; its members, known as Senderistas, strove for anarchy so they could impose their own dogma on the people. And they came perilously close to succeeding. They operated with a fixed top-down committee structure and set out to take Peru, village by village, peasant by peasant. Guzmán stated that "the masses have to be taught through overwhelming acts so that ideas can be pounded into them. . . . The masses in the nation need the leadership of a Communist party; we hope with more revolutionary theory and practice, with more armed actions, with more people's war, with more power, to reach the very heart of the class and the people and really win them over. Why? In order to serve them—that is what we want."[28]

In its efforts to pound ideas into the masses, Sendero killed some 30,000 persons, primarily campesinos (peasants), in its war of terror. In response, the military unleashed an all-out assault on suspected Senderistas, killing many innocent people. As a result, Peru had one of the world's worst human rights records. Andean women and men were caught in the middle. Many men fled the mountainous regions, where battles were first waged, to avoid conscription by Sendero or by the military. Liable to be executed by the military if they fed the Senderistas, the campesinos also lived in fear of torture or execution by Sendero if they assisted the military.

Survival Organizations

The social disorder and economic collapse caused by the seemingly endless war between Sendero and the military pushed more women, already challenged by poverty, to get involved with groups dedicated to solving the most basic survival problems. These women organized and worked in grassroots associations, like the *comedores populares,* the communal kitchens, and *Vaso de Leche* (Glass of Milk), in which the women were responsible for the acquisition, preparation, and delivery of milk to the barrios so that each child could have at least one cup of milk a day. In these organizations, the women used democratic practices, and many of them also honed their leadership skills.

As Sendero moved from rural villages into urban areas, the women who continued to participate in survival organizations showed great courage. In her 1992 report, prepared for the Women's Rights Project of Human Rights Watch, Robin Kirk revealed the degree to which Peruvian women had been abused in the war between the Peruvian military and Sendero. She wrote that rape was a regular tactic employed by members of the military: "Not only forced sex is involved. The central element of rape by the security forces is power. Soldiers use rape as a weapon: to punish, intimidate, coerce, humiliate and degrade."[29] The military responded to the charges of rape by saying that there had been occasional and regrettable excesses. One general tried to soften the nature of these excesses by explaining that "these boys are far from their families and suffer a great deal of tension because of the nature of combat."[30]

Race played a role in the selection of victims. White men in the military raped *cholas,* a term used for Indian women that is considered disparaging when used by non-Indians. Indians did not rape white women. Whites and mestizos—men of mixed Indian and Spanish background—raped mestizas and Indian women in detention. According to Kirk, Indian women received the most brutal treatment. They were likely to be raped "en masse," but mestizas were raped individually. Kirk and her investigators reported several instances where a light-skinned officer raped first, followed by those who were darker skinned, in accordance with their rank. *Tumbachola* refers to the knocking down and raping of an Indian woman; it also happens to be a barroom joke.[31]

Sendero leadership prohibited the raping of women. Instead, Senderista men intimidated women through death threats and the murders of key activists, as warnings to those who continued to work with organizations Sendero opposed. They murdered instead of raping the women who did not obey them.

In Kirk's opinion, Sendero targeted women because of their activism and not because of their gender, but I don't think gender should be eliminated as a factor. Women who did not acknowledge Sendero's authority made especially attractive targets, maybe more attractive than the men who resisted. Could there have been a special sweetness in "taking out" an uppity woman? Sendero wanted a foothold in the organizations run by women; it demanded collaboration, food, medicine, or a place to meet. Sendero also targeted those who fought for women's rights. It viewed feminism as part of an international conspiracy to divert the revolution.

Senderista women were also expected to follow orders. They were given the opportunity to prove themselves by administering the coup de grace in the killings of local authorities, police, and military officers. They also gave the fatal shot in public executions.[32] Despite the fact that Senderista women served in leadership positions, they still pleased the men to whom they reported by engaging in deplorable activities, characterized by the men as honorable.

As clear evidence of their adoption of violence as a tactic, Sendero spokesperson Luis Arce Borja told journalists: "We know that many innocent people are dying. But history is written with blood. We will never attain power if we are tormented by the deaths. The price is high, but without bloodshed and violence, there is no revolution. Our objective is to seize power. Only then will the deaths cease."[33]

The Assassination of María Elena

For her defiance of Sendero, María Elena Moyano was assassinated on February 15, 1992. She was only thirty-three years old. Thomas Kamm described what happened after María Elena was shot: "A group of rebels pulled her to a square in full view of the other attendees—including her two children—placed five kilos of dynamite under her and blew her up. 'Hurrah for the just sanction to the imperialist, counterrevolutionary agent, the recalcitrant, revisionist, and traitorous María Elena Moyano!,' Shining Path wrote in a leaflet."[34]

María Elena had said that any moral courage she possessed had been inspired by the women who worked with her to foment positive and peaceful change. These were the women whose very lives were a repudiation of an authoritarian, militaristic government and the rabid response to that government by Sendero.

Suspension of the Constitution

Even though Guzmán, Sendero's leader, was captured and imprisoned in September 1992, the poor of Peru, with little faith in the leaders and institutions that govern, continued to endure a grinding economic existence. On April 5, 1992, President Alberto Fujimori had disbanded Congress, fired all congressmen, and suspended the constitution—an action referred to as a self-coup by Peruvians and justified by Fujimori as the only way to stop Sendero. He then made an even tighter alliance with the military. According to Efraín Gonzales de Olarte, senior research associate at the North-South Center at the University of Miami, "contemporary Peru lives a fundamental contradiction: on the one hand, it is a nearly ungovernable country as a result of the weakness of its institutions; but, on the other hand, it is a country that is easy to lead as a result of deep social disintegration, which nearly precludes resistance to any action taken by government."[35]

Voters showed their approval of Fujimori's strong hand by approving a new constitution in a fall 1993 referendum. Women activists disapproved of the new constitution because it abandoned the prohibition against sexual discrimination. Additionally, in their opinion, Peruvians had paid a very high price when they lost the democratic structure of their government, with the firing of their representatives and the suspension of the constitution. They claimed that during the period when Fujimori claimed complete control, and while Guzmán was in prison, hundreds of individuals were summarily arrested or executed, many of whom might have been innocent. Others did not give credit to Fujimori because they argued that the antiterrorist unit that succeeded in capturing Guzmán existed before his presidency.[36]

Reelection of Fujimori

On April 9, 1995, Peruvians—weary of war, relieved to be able to walk on the streets without fear of death by a Sendero car bomb, and hopeful that the macroeconomic growth the country was experiencing would trickle down to them—confirmed Fujimori as president for five more years.

But little has trickled down to the poor. There have been insufficient allocations for education, health, and nutrition programs and too few social services. Poor women have had no alternative but to expend their energies trying to help their families survive. And many have had to do this in the face of abandonment or abuse by their husbands. In the last twenty years, female-headed households have grown and now represent 25 percent of households in many Latin American countries.[37]

Nongovernmental Organizations and Democracy

Workers in nongovernmental organizations (NGOs) are finally realizing that there can be no democracy when one-half of the population is disenfranchised. There is a connection between a woman's level of education and her degree of civic participation. There is also a correlation between a woman's educational achievement and the age at which she marries, the number of children she has, the health and life expectancy of her children, and the educational levels her children attain. Women's education is pivotal in the overall democratic development of a country.[38]

Some NGOs investigated the coordinators and beneficiaries of their own programs, in response to the paltry distribution of economic growth to the poor. In a 1993 report published by the Among Women South-North Dialogue, researchers found that 80 percent of the projects were "oriented toward men and women without distinction, without any specific attention to women."[39]

Professionals who work in international development efforts had been using the term "women in development" or "women and development" when they dealt with technical training or other opportunities for women. The concept behind this language, however, accepted the subordinate position of women in society. The development workers unwittingly reinforced women's societal roles and didn't question the traditional division of labor. "Gender and development," on the other hand, reflects the understanding that the roles of men and women in society are interdependent. This framework acknowledges the existence of discrimination against women, but it encompasses men too. It also facilitates an analysis of the various forms of subordination and discrimination women experience through the variables of age, race, socioeconomic background, sexual preference, and geographical location.[40]

Flora Tristán, a Peruvian NGO

Since its founding in 1979, the Flora Tristán Center for the Peruvian Woman has become one of the most influential NGOs in Peru, providing a standard for other women's NGOs throughout Latin America.[41] It was named for Flora Tristán Moscoso, the Paris-born woman who is now recognized as having helped lay the groundwork for modern feminist theory. Tristán, daughter of a French mother and a Peruvian father, had visited Peru during 1833 and 1834. She believed that the emancipation of women was inextricably related to the emancipation of the worker.[42]

While there was great merit in Tristán's premise, we know now that women continue to suffer inequities in the workplace, even after their male counterparts have been "emancipated." To make matters worse, the economic crisis in the nineties caused the labor field for women to shrink. At the same time, women's organizations in Peru lost some of their strategic positions. Social deterioration diminished their ability to respond to social necessities, to relate to other institutions, to mentor women regarding participation in public life, and to negotiate effectively.[43]

In response to these circumstances, the members of Flora Tristán set the following goals. This NGO will (1) ensure that women's interests are considered in political decisions; (2) make visible women's contributions to society to ensure that their interests are represented in development plans; (3) support the entry of women into political life; (4) oppose the violation of their human rights and achieve full recognition of and exercise of these rights in society; and (5) secure the reproductive and sexual rights of women.

To achieve these objectives, the members operate seven programs. The

Women's Rights Program promotes the civic life of women and advances their fundamental rights at the regional and national levels. The Health and Reproductive Rights Program encourages women to take ownership of their own health and educates them as to their reproductive rights. It coordinates its activities with the Ministry of Health. The National Rural Women's Network provides education to men and women to improve the effectiveness and impact of their work and to strengthen communication between them. It advises organizations and businesses of gender considerations in the application of their strategies. The program coordinates the Andean Rural Women's Network, active in Peru, Ecuador, and Bolivia, which focuses on food technology. The Investigation Program is academically oriented and is responsible for the study and development of gender theory, including the phenomena of subordination and inequality of women. The Communication Program helps to inform public opinion and political decision-making. It promotes activities that modify stereotypical images of women in the mass media. As one of its dissemination strategies, it organizes campaigns and contests. Open to the public, the Flora Tristán Library houses the most complete collection in Peru of books that deal with the theme of women. The Editorial Program edits and distributes the center's publications. It promotes creativity in women by publishing their work and organizes the Magda Portal story contest in Latin America.[44]

To understand the turmoil that has affected Flora Tristán during the last decade, one must be keenly aware of the danger and threats of danger that have impacted every dimension of the organization. For example, many women at Flora Tristán knew and worked with María Elena Moyano, whose 1992 assassination by Sendero Luminoso stunned them and had a disastrous effect on their outreach programs.

Gender Theory and the Heterogeneity of Women

Another major challenge facing Flora Tristán and the overall women's movement in Latin America is the need to construct a gender identity that encompasses the heterogeneity of women. Virginia Vargas calls for the expression of the diverse voices of women—voices of the urban and rural poor, migrants, students, workers, mothers, single women, and professionals. The experiences of women from all walks of life should be "ransomed" to develop a female consciousness and to avoid splitting the movement into segments defined by role or class.[45]

Vargas emphasizes the importance of understanding the Latin American past in the construction of gender theory. She invites women to turn their eyes "toward the footprints of the conquest and of colonization, to the subordination of the peasant woman, to the enslavement of the black woman, to the historical isolation of the middle class woman, . . . to the historical burden of the traditional church; in summary, to the marks that all of these have left on the body and mind of this heterogeneous category of women."[46]

Women who have systematically been left out of the analysis of women's social movements must be included in the development of gender theory. References to racial subordination, for example, do not adequately establish the connections between race and gender. Vargas mentions Lelia González, a black Brazilian feminist, who stated that both racism and sexism have their origins in biology, and that women, according to "the basic domination ideology" on the South American continent, are assumed to be of unequal social value. She urges that the connections between race and gender be made clear to avoid a Eurocentric and neocolonialist perspective. According to González, feminists who have pushed the issue of gender subordination have made an abstraction of the racial issue, making it difficult to develop viable proposals in multiracial and multicultural societies, and thus "distorting the history and reality of thousands of women."[47]

Lesbians, too, have been on the periphery of the movement in Latin America. Some are leaving the closet, however, and are embracing the women's movement—an extraordinarily difficult undertaking because of the authoritarian and conservative nature of their society. Feminist groups have only recently opened their doors to lesbians, doors previously closed because of feminists' fears they all would be considered lesbians by an ignorant public. On the relationship between lesbians and feminists, Vargas writes, "If we have maintained, as a principle, the right to be different, the right to our own bodies, it is unjust that this be valid for some and not for others."[48]

Machismo

If Latin American women are to succeed in their quest for full citizenship, the cultural phenomenon of machismo must be weakened through education that increases awareness of what democracy requires. *Cassell's Spanish-English Dictionary* has two entries for *macho*. The first lists "a male animal or plant; a part of any instrument which enters into another; a tool for cutting female screw-threads; a male screw; a hook to catch hold in an eye; a bolt (of a lock), a spur, a buttress, an abutment; a sledge hammer; a block in which an anvil is fixed; a square anvil and an *ignorant fellow*" (emphasis mine). The second definition lists the adjectives "male, masculine, robust, and vigorous." Unfortunately, Spanish does not have an equivalent word, without negative connotations, to describe a woman who is robust and vigorous. In Latin America, *macho* frequently connotes a man's control over women. Women who don't speak Spanish also recognize the behavior patterns that have given rise to the term's widespread use. Wherever it occurs, machismo is antithetical to democracy, because it assumes the superiority and dominance of one-half of the human species and denies a voice to women who might construct reality differently than men.

In Latin America, machismo, according to Elizabeth Jelin, combines with another cultural phenomenon, that of "the cult of the dedicated and suffering mother."[49] The cultural norm that honorable women should bear their husbands' or partners' infidelities or abuse with silent stoicism, or privately suffer oppression at home or in the workplace, is not easily displaced. It is frequently tied to an abhorrence of giving a name (and thereby reality) to practices that violate women's sexuality. The women's movement has done much to name the violations and to create the awareness that must develop if changes are to be achieved.

The Goals for Feminists

In the latter half of the nineties, many Latin American feminists strove for the elimination of sexual hierarchies, and, in Vargas's strong language, they sought "a subversion of the patriarchal order."[50] They looked for a reality "that considers the women's perspective and a plan for an alternative to existing society based on equality in relationships among human beings, where discrimination by sex, race, class or age has no place."[51]

The future of democracy, then, is intertwined with the development of democratic relationships within the family, workplace, and state. This goal will remain elusive until women recognize their own complicity in accepting men's power, and Vargas cautions that most of the spaces into which women are trying to develop their personal and professional potential have already been defined by men. She calls for resistance to the dynamics of oppression and an articulation of these dynamics, to bring them into the open. What is especially insidious to the movement is that women frequently do not see the "patriarchal reality" in these institutions.[52]

Based on her intimate knowledge of the women's movement in Latin America, Vargas offers the following goals for feminists.

(1) Go where the women are and expand the definition of what it means to be a feminist. Vargas reminds feminists who believe they are the vanguard to stop measuring the level of other women's feminist consciousness. She reminds us that we are all searching for more democratic relationships, and that the many personal and professional spaces we occupy represent fertile opportunities to strengthen the movement.

(2) Make connections between and among the issues. Keep such issues as the relationships between the sexes and health alive, for example, but point out the connections between domestic violence and a violence-prone society, daily subsistence and food policies, reproduction rights and public policy.

(3) Look for new spaces to conquer while consolidating your own spaces to avoid isolation of the struggle and the reproduction of separate spaces for women. Avoid deepening the segregation between masculine and feminine spaces. There is a real concern that those women who work to secure the basic needs of their communities—like food, shelter, and health—through their voluntary organizational work will contribute to this segregation and add to the burdens they already have. It would be detrimental to women if these services were viewed as their exclusive domain, thus spreading the segregation of work in the home to the public sector. Furthermore, there is the fear that government will wash its hands of its social and humanitarian responsibilities as women assume these tasks.

(4) Extract all of the political consequences from the recognition of all the roles that women inhabit. For example, the need for child care and social security for women who work with or without remuneration.

(5) Beware of feminism that is self-sufficient or complacent, that finds' its reason for existence in itself and in its own spaces, not risking confrontation with patriarchal power.[53]

In the years before her death, María Elena Moyano chose to confront rather than ignore or recoil from patriarchal power. She died because she stood up to Sendero's threats and its use of terrorism, the most grisly manifestations of patriarchal power.

María Elena Moyano

The Life and Death of a Peruvian Activist

In this part of the prologue, I use, as a guide, the sequence of the original work, *María Elena Moyano: En busca de una esperanza.* Part One opened with María Elena's description of the "dirty war" that poor Peruvians endured during the eighties and early nineties, the human rights abuses that included atrocities against women, and the people's disenchantment with politics and politicians. The exceptions she noted were the grassroots, community-run organizations, like the communal kitchen and Vaso de Leche programs. The women who worked in these democratically run organizations had to go head-to-head with local and state officials to solve issues related to survival. It is here that María Elena first referred to machismo as the "grave societal problem that women in Peru face."

Villa El Salvador

María Elena revealed her love and respect for the valorous people of Villa El Salvador, the *pueblo joven* that was formed in 1973 and became home to 300,000 people by the time of her death. Starting as a shantytown, with no water or electricity, Villa El Salvador (Villa) had earned an international reputation for the active role its inhabitants played in its governance and development. Pope John Paul II had celebrated Mass in Villa when he visited Peru in 1985. María Elena offered Villa as an example of how an organized people can secure rights from the state. (In January 1993, during the visit of then secretary-general of the United Nations Javier Pérez de Cuellar, it earned the appellation "Messenger City of Peace and Development.")

The Popular Women's Federation of Villa El Salvador (FEPOMUVES)

María Elena described how the most well-known and effective women's organizations in Peru got started, and the role the Popular Women's Federation of Villa El Salvador (FEPOMUVES) and other women's organizations have played in women's growing political participation and in the development of their confidence and skills. The Women's Federation ultimately became the coordinating agency for the activities of all the women's organizations in this very large municipality and the impetus behind health, human rights, and political campaigns. Members moved beyond survival issues to an integrated development plan.

Fulfillment of Basic Needs

María Elena admitted that the primary concern of the women with whom she lived and worked was their families. Although she acknowledged the feminist fear that their communal work might extend the traditional, domestic, sexual division of labor found in the home to the public sphere, she stood firmly in support of the accomplishments of the women who organized, operated, and staffed these programs. The work had to be done. Did it make sense for the women to abandon their feeding programs because it made more work for them and excused the men and government from these tasks?

She characterized the Vaso de Leche program (which distributed powdered milk donated from the United States) as a major achievement of Peru's United Left Party. Rather than creating a new entity to administer the program, the then-mayor of Lima, Alfonso Barrantes Lingán, used the existing Women's Federation to coordinate the program. María Elena also answered the criticism that the programs she supported robbed the people of initiative. She explained the role these programs play in self-government.

Programs directed at easing the plight of the poor, however, especially those that required government cooperation, like the Vaso de Leche program, were anathema to Sendero, because they diminished grievances against the government and were thought to lessen revolutionary fervor among the poor. The women who refused to be cowed by Sendero's threats and continued to manage Vaso de Leche centers became primary targets for the terrorists. In September 1991, Sendero planted a bomb in one of the milk distribution centers and blamed María Elena for the episode. María Elena countered with her own declaration against Sendero, pointing out the absurdity of its charges and the futility of its tactics.

Women began the communal kitchens to stave off hunger and malnutrition in their families. They pooled their labor, utensils, food, and cooking skills. In addition to evaluating the quality of their food, the women evaluated the quality of their relationships. María Elena recognized that women couldn't stop with the filling of stomachs. Hunger was only a symptom of the problems they faced.

The Economic Crisis and "Women's Work"

The economic crisis, worsened by the policies of three successive administrations, had a broad and sweeping effect on women, leaving them more marginalized than ever. Women with children, in particular, found it harder to carry out the multitude of responsibilities that fell to them alone: procuring food, water, and fuel; cooking; doing the laundry; performing duties relating to their children's health and education; undertaking activities to supplement their income—to name a few.

The economic adjustments that bankrupt countries must make to secure loans diminish the funds available for nutrition, health, and educational programs that might assist these women. Moreover, the ranks of those who ask for help from the government grow as resources become scarcer. But María Elena pointed out that the new competitors for government assistance didn't have the organizing and practical experience the women had. It was the women who knew how to fight. In 1990, when Fujimori launched the austerity program that became known as "Fujishock," the women demanded that there be "shock for the rich and not for the poor." María Elena noted the positive impact the Women's Federation had had in easing the shock on the poor in her district through its 1,500 Vaso de Leche committees and its 800 communal kitchens.

María Elena Runs for Political Office

When the women in the federation realized they had become marginalized, even within the political parties of the left, they looked to María

Elena, because her experience made her the logical candidate to run for public office.

With women's growing clout in organizational life, men began to recognize their value in getting out the voters, but they showed little interest in backing the women for serious political positions, so the Women's Federation decided to run its own candidate, María Elena. The United Left Party subsequently invited her to be its candidate for deputy mayor but not mayor. María Elena and the federation accepted. The women of the federation campaigned zealously for her, and by the time of the election, more people knew what she stood for than they knew of the male candidate for mayor.

Helpful, of course, was the fact that the people were already familiar with the many other campaigns waged by the Women's Federation: health and education campaigns that provided diagnostic services for vaginal infections and cervical cancer; public information campaigns regarding the dangers of cholera and how to prevent contagion; drives against domestic violence; and environmental and drug awareness education programs. And always, the women created awareness about the struggle for their rights within the social structure of machismo. Although absent at higher levels of government—as aldermen, for example—they continued to question existing political structures, giving voice to the women they represented.

María Elena envisioned women participating in all decisions taken by municipal government and, in the long run, at all levels of national representation. She even dared to consider placing a woman in the executive office.

Community Protection Committees

As the government showed itself to be ever weaker before the demands of international lenders and spread out more thinly in response to armed revolution, it was poor women who assumed the responsibility for making their communities safe and clean. They also wrangled with merchants to keep prices down. They monitored the stores in their communities and brought pressure on shopkeepers who gouged or horded goods to sell at a high price later when goods would be scarce. The women organized neighborhood defense committees to defend themselves against Sendero violence and to ward off drug commerce. They expected vendors in the markets to keep their areas clean and to handle food in a hygienic way. They demonstrated keen civic-mindedness, a concern for the common good. These women were building democracy from the bottom up, while pressuring government to respond from the top down.

María Elena Confronts Sendero Luminoso, the Military, and Police

Sendero labeled María Elena a "revisionist" who "manipulates women." It accused her of helping the government. María Elena recalled how, during the early years, she thought Sendero was fighting for justice and was on the side of the people. She admitted her mistake and was puzzled by its approach, which undermined the people's own organizations and increased their suffering. María Elena chastised the left for having abandoned the people, believing that an organized left was the only force capable of defeating Sendero, because people had no confidence in the right. She explained that some individuals had given up on the left and had joined this militant, violent group as an alternative; she held the left partly responsible for the success Sendero enjoyed.

María Elena disparaged the Peruvian government's feeble attempts to stem violence in the country, while crediting the women in the community organizations for giving her the courage she needed to confront Sendero. Sendero's tactic of killing labor and community leaders and of terrorizing the women by planting a bomb in a Vaso de Leche center prompted María Elena to take a public stand against it. She accused the group of attacking the organizations of the poor and of increasing the levels of malnutrition and death. Vowing that Sendero would not close the communal kitchens, she asked where mothers would feed their families if not in the kitchens. She called upon women to dispel the fear provoked by Sendero, and stated that Senderistas were no longer revolutionaries but terrorists. She acknowledged the victory against Sendero must be more than a military defeat because its cause was ideological.

The police were not exempt. María Elena accused them of violence and murder, saying that before the people could regain their faith in the police, the police would have to "bring about justice with the disappeared, tortured, imprisoned, and assassinated."

María Elena surmised that she could be a target of Sendero but added that she had faith, and that she hoped the women of Lima (better off economically) would join in her cause once they realized what was happening in the rural areas and outlying municipalities. She, nonetheless, stated she was ready to surrender her life.

Previous Assassinations of Women Activists

She had good reason to be contemplating her own death. Between 1985 and 1991, three women who were active in survival groups were murdered, including María Antenati Hilario de Olympia and Margarita Astride de la Cruz. The attack that first gained public attention, however, was the killing of Juana López on August 31, 1991. She had previously received written threats from Sendero, demanding that she leave her post with the Vaso de Leche center in Callao, a major port city near Lima. An envelope containing a bullet was hand-delivered to her home. A few days later she was killed while ladling out milk to recipients at the center. María Elena began receiving death threats two weeks after López's death.

On December 6, 1991, terrorists killed Doraliza Espejo Márquez, another Vaso de Leche coordinator, who had earlier mobilized a march to protest terror in the large *pueblo joven* of San Juan de Lurigancho. Four men and a woman came to her door under the pretext of signing up for the milk program. Instead, they shot her three times and left a sign that read, "This is how traitors who collaborate with the army die."[1]

Just before Christmas, on December 20, 1991, Emma Hilario, director of the National Commission of Communal Kitchens, was in her home with her husband and brother when five gunmen opened fire on the home. Hilario and her relatives miraculously survived. One year earlier, she had received the "Angel Escobar" award from Peru's Human Rights Coordinating Committee for her work with the National Commission on Communal Kitchens, which represented nine thousand kitchens throughout Peru.[2] María Elena wrote to her, demonstrating her compassion and solidarity, reminding her that the two of them really had no place to hide, that she couldn't tell Hilario to be careful because, in the end, no one was going to protect them.

María Elena Throws Down the Gauntlet

Once she was chosen as a target, Sendero maligned María Elena in a widely distributed pamphlet. In her rebuttal document, María Elena answered every charge leveled against her. Sendero said she was allied with the government and the armed forces. She replied that she had always fought against oppressive governments and against their human rights abuses. Sendero accused her of forming urban patrols in her community that assisted the military. María Elena responded that the urban patrols had been part of the history of her community, that they had been autonomous, and that they dealt with local problems like delinquency and drug addiction. She was charged with stealing from the people. María Elena described her long history of volunteer labor in the areas of literacy and health. She pointed to her efforts in Villa, where she worked tirelessly, without remuneration, to help build its infrastructure. She was accused of stealing money from various agencies, but she denied these charges, explaining that the money in question was administered by others, and that there were documents proving she had handled it properly. Finally, Sendero accused her of the most ludicrous of all the charges—that of dynamiting the Vaso de Leche distribution center. Unself-consciously, she reiterated her identification with social justice causes and said, "I could never destroy what I have built with my own hands."

Finally, she wrested the revolution from Sendero: The women of the popular classes were the true revolutionaries, who would change Peruvian society in a revolution of "individual and collective dignity." She urged her neighbors to believe in and fight for a "just and dignified society." María Elena and her neighbors would participate in the transition toward democracy through the organizations they had created.

María Elena threw down the gauntlet by organizing a women's march against terror. She called upon women to defend the fruits of their labor. Where were the people to go if they couldn't look to government or the military to solve this crisis of terror? People were also fed up with Peruvian political parties. In these circumstances, it is the "people who must confront Sendero." Again, she reminded the people that the campaign should be political and not military. She called for a "contest of goals" and asked, "What is it we want to build?" She noted that the people were fighting

from a weakened position because their government had stopped supporting the community organizations that helped them survive.

The women's organizations were under economic threat from the government, and their members were under bodily threat from Sendero. The
women had told Sendero that it couldn't hope to change the country
through violence and terror, by assassinating the leaders of the people and
killing the priests who worked among them. María Elena drove home the
point that it wouldn't be the Senderistas who changed the country, but the
people "who learn to take charge of their own destinies." She admitted
that the general public had not yet reacted to the threats of violence, because they had not yet been touched by them. María Elena rejected Senderistas as *compañeros* who fought for the people: "They fight against the
people," she said.

María Elena outlined the box in which these poor people lived. On one
side was the economic crisis that was crushing them. The second side of
the box was Sendero, whose members annihilated community leaders and
wanted to impose their dogma on the entire country. The military force
that violated human rights was side three, and side four was the government's neoliberal economic policies that further restricted the options of
the poor.

Meanwhile, Sendero was closing in on Lima, and it was the *pueblos
jóvenes,* with their community organizations, run by courageous and
proud civilians, that stood between Sendero and the rest of Lima. Vaso de
Leche and the communal kitchens were in jeopardy. The women com-
prised the vanguard against the neighborhood incursions of Sendero, and
they used active nonviolence to resist. María Elena wanted to formalize
this resistance through district accords that would unite those who "favor
peace and democracy" over "war and death."

It is likely that the diminution of violence and terror after the September
1992 capture of Guzmán, Sendero's leader, was due not only to President
Fujimori's crackdown but also to the activism of María Elena, to the general shock in response to her murder, and to the other women activists
who risked their lives by their indefatigable truth-telling about Sendero.
The 300,000 people who marched behind María Elena's coffin were fed
up with Sendero. María Elena's murder and the assassinations of other
brave women might have finally awakened those who had been on the
periphery of the struggle, leaving Sendero without a foothold.

María Elena's Autobiography

In Part Two of the original work, María Elena shared the early, happy memories when she was together with both her parents. She and her siblings moved with their mother to desertlike Villa El Salvador after their home in Surco, a pleasant Lima neighborhood, was taken (presumably for economic reasons) and their furniture seized. They built their new, humble house with their own hands. Señora Moyano played a significant role in advancing her children's education while she laundered clothes to pay their expenses.

María Elena's girlhood years revolved around school and church activities. She and her six siblings knew hunger, but they also had creative outlets and participated in musical theater and religious dramas. In one such drama, María Elena played the role of Mary Magdalene, a precursor of the role she would later play—a woman feared and shunned by the ideologically righteous, but an apostle to the people, as Mary Magdalene had been *the* apostle to the apostles.

María Elena wanted to be a secretary; her mother insisted she study law. With her brothers' support and the encouragement of her fiancé, Gustavo, María Elena applied to Garcilaso de la Vega University to study sociology. While attending the university, she was one of many youths who gathered at a local hall to socialize and to discuss their concerns. In addition to reflecting upon the Bible, they talked about the dangers of drugs and about communication problems with their parents. She spoke of their "Christian convictions," of their loyalty to community, and of their desire to contribute.

Soon María Elena met some older youths who told her that the Bible was not going to solve the problems of the poor. María Elena defended her group's efforts, replying that love and unity are an effective way to begin. She began to study Marx and to question the perpetual condition of poverty in which she, her family, and her neighbors lived. How could God allow so many children to die from hunger? In informal groups María Elena and others studied about the Chinese revolution and class struggle. She decided she no longer believed in God and eventually turned toward socialism.

The group leaders believed it was time to start an experimental school for the members' children and chose María Elena to direct it. She felt proud and excited to have become a teacher so easily, and her confidence grew. Although bare-bones, the first nonformal, early education school (PRONOEI) began in Villa. Gradually, other classrooms opened, and the young women studied instructional methods as well as the curriculum used by the state Ministry of Education.

These idealistic women worked as volunteers. At the time their male mentors asked them to start these schools, they thought it inappropriate to think of salaries. They believed the small children from their communities needed a jump start on their educations to compensate for their surroundings. Gradually, the teachers realized that others, with equivalent educations, were paid for their efforts. The educational workers' union solicited the nonformal teachers to participate in its strike. María Elena joined wholeheartedly and participated in the occupation of a school, keeping watch and even gathering stones as weapons.

María Elena was full of exuberance in her early twenties. She had a keen sense of what was unjust in her community and identified closely with those who had similar convictions. Some of her activities, however, contradicted her ideology, as when, for example, in order to pay her university fees, she filled in for striking teachers in the public schools. The strike fizzled; the state replaced hundreds of teachers; some of her friends ended up in prison, and María Elena was frustrated. She found solace with Gustavo, her companion of five years and fiancé.

Using language that feminists would disdain, María Elena "surrendered" to Gustavo to have a baby. She had yearned for a child and wanted to be the ideal mother. Pregnant, she also wanted her child to have an exemplary father, but she did not want to pressure Gustavo into marrying her because he had his own financial obligations, and she didn't want to further burden him. Jobless, sick from the pregnancy, she was dependent upon her mother and brothers, who were no longer understanding and supportive. Where were her friends now that she was pregnant, had lost her job, and had withdrawn from the university?

María Elena was a traditional woman in that she wanted a monogamous relationship with her companion, wanted a baby, and wanted a healthy family life for her baby. She was thinking nontraditionally when she entertained the idea of raising her child without the economic help of the father. Like a traditional woman, she put Gustavo's needs before her own, but her mother had other ideas and asked Gustavo to marry her daughter. Because María Elena's mother had been too poor to have had a traditional wedding, she was adamant that her daughter would be married in white.

While pregnant, María Elena lived with the macho criticism of her brothers; the apparent futility of her activism; the loss of her job; withdrawal from the university; the determined will of her mother; the awareness of her growing vulnerability as a pregnant woman; and deep concern for the father of her developing baby—all within the context of poverty.

Through the sacrifices made by her entire family, she was able to have a traditional wedding in the church where she had been baptized. But as she walked down the aisle, she recalled the young strikers and wondered if she had abandoned them and her "people's revolutionary struggle." Like many women, she was torn between personal fulfillment and her perceived obligations to others. She married and would have a child before knowing who she was or what her role in life would be.

Wanting to be a good wife, she temporarily set aside her revolutionary activities. She gave her husband the best food, eating whatever was left, but he didn't like her cooking, and so she cried. They fought; she felt subordinate to him. She gave birth to her first son in her mother's bed, attended by a midwife and her husband, and felt the boundless joy many women feel upon the birth of their first child.

Economic pressures forced the newlyweds to become custodians at an apartment building in Miraflores, one of Lima's better neighborhoods. María Elena felt isolated; she was with strangers, the majority of whom were from Peru's criollo class. Who were these people who wouldn't even greet her? One of the tenants accused María Elena's family of stealing items from a clothesline. María Elena was disgusted by this expression of class discrimination and expressed her pent-up rage at the rich woman who had made the accusation. She returned to Villa, got two part-time teaching positions, and helped to found a mothers' club that she directed for three years.

It was in this local mothers' club that María Elena's concerns for social justice became focused on women. She became aware of their marginalization in Peruvian society. She realized that even her own husband behaved in a macho fashion. They had more fights because she wanted him to assume more household duties.

Eventually, María Elena became active in the Popular Women's Federation of Villa El Salvador (FEPOMUVES) and was elected undersecretary. This involvement marked a new stage in her personal life and in her development as a civic leader. She was elected president of the federation in 1986 and was reelected to a second term in 1988.

María Elena participated in a series of public forums in which she protested the violent tactics of Sendero and pleaded for the group to end the violence. Her friends convinced her that her life was in danger. She briefly left the country and upon her return, requested and received two police bodyguards. At the end of 1991, *La República,* one of Peru's leading newspapers, named her "Personality of the Year."[3]

On February 14, 1992, María Elena unequivocally protested the armed strike that Sendero had called on that day. She led a march in Villa El Salvador, where participants carried white banners, signifying peace. The day after, she was gunned down at a fund-raising meal for a women's group.

In simple, poemlike notes, written a few days before her death, María Elena revisited her life as one who knew she would soon die, glimpsing life's beauty and tragedy in swiftly passing images. These notes reveal the profundity of her love for her husband and children, the women with whom she struggled, and life itself. She mourned the loss of a fellow activist who had been murdered; expressed gratefulness for her family and for the tender love she shared with Gustavo; wrote of the fragility of life and of her impotence before the force of those who do not love.

She also acknowledged the source of the richness and fullness of her life: "My God, how I've lived. Thank you for giving me so much! Love, the opportunity to give my all—everything." As a child she had been influenced by the most humane principles of her church; as a university student, she abandoned formal religious practice, and, at one point, admitted to having become an atheist. Nevertheless, she died upholding the most edifying and essential ingredients of that church—justice and dignity for the poor, and the willingness to give one's life for one's neighbor. Her theology had been liberated. One can draw parallels between her life and that of Jesus Christ, parallels which some critics will find unseemly: she lived in poverty, had a short public life, and died for her people at age thirty-three.

Part One

All photos were provided by Diana Miloslavich Tupac and the Flora Tristán Center for the Peruvian Woman, Lima, Peru. Most of these photos were previously used in the editions published in Peru and in Spain. The translator also acknowledges the co-operation of the documentation center at *La República*.

1. María Elena Moyano. Photo by Cristina Hee, from *María Elena Moyano: En busca de una esperanza* (Peru).

I

Peru
In Search of Hope

> I come from the young town of Villa El Salvador. I want to describe briefly to you what my country is enduring.

Peru is a country with many problems, problems of a political, social, economic, and moral nature; problems that involve each and every one of the structures of the state.

We are living a dirty war. In the name of democracy, women are being violated; community leaders are being detained; entire towns are being obliterated. One faction says it fights for the people but assassinates community leaders and imposes its ideas through force, using authoritarian means and terror.

The circumstances that surround Peru are complex. The results of the last elections, for example, provided some big surprises. The politicians made repeated promises, but the people didn't believe them. The people, wanting to express their needs and opinions, voted for some unknown politician [Alberto Fujimori] and, in the end, were still betrayed.[1]

In the last few years, women have proven how effective grassroots political participation can be. We have not participated merely to register opposition, complain about our lives, or simply denounce others. We have documented our complaints and have struggled to offer concrete proposals and alternatives for solving each of our problems.

This participation has been very effective in alleviating hunger and misery. Women have organized communal kitchens—hundreds and thousands of them—and Vaso de Leche committees. These programs have made it possible for a woman to leave the confines of her home to work in a new, public space. There, she deals with issues of nutrition, survival, social conflict, personal problems, and gender issues, such as domestic violence, when she is beaten and mistreated by her companion.

Women have had to engage in constant battles with local and state political officials. Their involvement in these matters has been effective throughout the capital. When, for example, the budget for Vaso de Leche was to be cut, women took action that had great political repercussions in the Lima metropolitan area. They were responsible for the passage of Bill 24059, which states that the country's overall budget must allocate funds to provide a glass of milk each day to all of the nation's children. Perhaps that seems like a simple matter, but for Peruvian children, a glass of milk is vital, because it can make the difference between life and death.

As a result of their struggle and grassroots efforts to develop alternative methods for solving the problems of survival, women have also had a major presence on the national political scene. Now the Vaso de Leche and communal kitchen programs cannot be threatened without provoking the women. Women must be consulted about these programs. They are ready to stand firm and struggle, even if it means going on strike to prevent other forces from deciding the fate of these programs.

There has been massive participation by women in survival issues. As a result, they have acquired high levels of political and personal consciousness about human rights and about machismo, the especially grave societal problem that women in Peru face. Yes, women have won many of their rights.

2. Shortly before her death, at a rally to protest the violence of Sendero Luminoso. From *María Elena Moyano, Perú en busca de una esperanza* (Spain).

II

Villa El Salvador
A Valorous Community

> Villa, I remember, as a little girl, that you were poor and had no electricity. Now everyone comments on your clean streets, filled with young people. In Villa I was born; in Villa I grew up; in Villa I studied; in Villa I fell in love. On the day I die and am buried, I shall leave my grave to fight for Villa.[2]

I learned so much in Villa El Salvador. It was a school, a place where many people, including leaders, were shaped. I also believe that, in a certain sense, Peru's hope lies in Villa.

Not too long ago, we suffered from lack of water and even shelter. At times the wind carried away our straw mats, and the sand that blew into our food did not permit us to eat. We withstood many hardships. But we learned much in the midst of this strife. For example, we learned about solidarity, a quality native to Villa El Salvador, that enables us to fight together. For me, those twenty years [since the founding of Villa El Salvador] represent the step-by-step construction of a new society.

Because of the organization, participation, and struggle of its people, Villa El Salvador is well known nationally and internationally.[3] The level of development we achieved in recent years has been sustained not by the state but by the participation of an organized people. That participation has been essential for the transformation of sandy soil into land that has been planted with thousands of trees. That participation caused schools to be built. And the participation of women was decisive in the building of Villa El Salvador.

Villa El Salvador is a concrete example of how a people can organize to secure certain rights from the state.[4] The Senderistas,[5] nevertheless, hope to destroy our very real accomplishments. We have brought together 2,500 local organizations, composed of youth, women, and small business owners. The Senderistas want to destroy our efforts. They tell us that our way is wrong. For them, the only way to change the state is by winning a "people's war." Our point of view is totally different.

3. During an interview. Photo by Carmen Charo, from
María Elena Moyano, Perú en busca de una esperanza.

III

The Popular Women's Federation of Villa El Salvador

In 1983 we founded the Popular Women's Federation
of Villa El Salvador.

An organizing committee was formed in 1979 to coordinate the women's
activities that were already under way in the district.[6] Communal kitchens, affiliated with churches, were emerging, and there were committees
responsible for the planting of trees. (Villa El Salvador has always been a
desert.) At that time, the planting of trees was very significant for the
community because trees give life, and those planting committees were
very active.

That same organizing committee was responsible for solving community problems. It organized women into groups and also opposed certain
conditions for assistance imposed by various philanthropic organizations.
For example, before giving the women food, these organizations stipu-
lated that they had to do community work and had to show up for work
between two and six in the afternoon. At times, there was nothing to do,
yet the women had to meet the obligation.

The mothers' clubs began in 1980. The government encouraged their
development, and these clubs received food assistance from the Adventist
Philanthropic Office for Social Action (OFASA), from the National Agrar-

ian Organization (ONA), and from other philanthropic organizations that imposed their respective conditions for communal labor.

At a 1981 meeting, all of the organizations receiving food assistance, together with the planting committees, decided to create a federation task force. Its major objective was to prevent the manipulation that accompanied the delivery of food and to provide us with a means by which we could offer suggestions to these donor institutions.

We made progress, and women's clubs with other objectives emerged. Objectives included the evaluation of women's roles and opportunities for training and empowerment. We also decided to study the problems of our community and the reasons underlying our poverty.

In 1983 we held the first women's convention in which the Popular Women's Federation of Villa El Salvador (FEPOMUVES) was created.[7] The federation was composed of seventy women's clubs. Each club represented what we call a residential group, comprising 384 families.

So that's how, in 1983, we began operating as a federation that had much wider objectives. The Vaso de Leche program, supported by the women's clubs, came later. There were many more communal kitchens, and more levels of organization. There was a group that worked for the defense of women's rights. Campaigns for legal and human rights were launched. Later the women gathered in sewing cooperatives to increase their income. Progress continued as a result of health, communication, and education workshops. Advertising campaigns emphasized the importance of women's health.

This history led to what the federation is today. Practically speaking, this autonomous federation has facilitated the centralization of all the activities of the women's movement in Lima. The federation is probably the only entity in all of Lima where this type of coordination occurs. In addition to the coordination of the activities of the organizations that deal with survival—the kitchens, Vaso de Leche committees, and women's clubs—we outlined a program that goes well beyond survival and is part of an integral development plan.

Women work at the industrial park and in other organizations like the Human Rights Committee. We at the federation continually evaluate Peru's political situation and respond in an organized way to problems at the national level.

I think women have made significant individual and collective gains. We see the high number of women who leave their homes to become involved in the community. Today there are thousands of leaders in Villa El Salvador who direct several types of activities. Before, involved only with their own families, they overlooked their skills. Women are now developing their talents and creativity within their own communities, through their own organizations. In this respect, I think women have made tremendous strides.

The primary concern of women continues to be their families, their children. It is the women who must leave home and join the community to survive; the priority of women from the poor classes is survival. As mothers, they know and feel that their children come first.

Certain people from various political persuasions have told us that we have traded domestic work for community labor. I don't think this is true. Yes, there is still a lack of outlets that provide wider opportunities for participation, but I believe that our organizations enable women to develop their skills, to study, to work for remuneration, while dedicating themselves to their children. Thus women carry out both responsibilities. They are overworked, perhaps, but also valued and empowered.[8]

4. At a demonstration in the Plaza San Martín, Lima. *La República*, from *María Elena Moyano: En busca de una esperanza.*

IV

The Vaso de Leche Program

> We have always been told that the kitchens and the Vaso de Leche committees put the people to sleep and serve as a mattress for the system. We say this is not so; instead we count on the people's capacity to govern themselves.

The Vaso de Leche program was the fruit of the labor of the United Left and of Dr. Alfonso Barrantes Lingán, during his term as mayor of Lima. It represents one of the few promises that this United Left candidate fulfilled.[9]

The federation already existed when Vaso de Leche emerged. Lima and Villa El Salvador respected our organization. They did not create a parallel unit to organize the milk distribution program but took advantage of the federation.

We promoted Vaso de Leche, each of us taking turns to make the program work. They gave us only raw milk; we had to use our own kettles, utensils, sugar, cinnamon, and clove [to make the milk more palatable]. We organized ourselves into small Vaso de Leche groups, under the auspices of the mothers' clubs that constituted the foundation of the federation.

In the First Metropolitan Convention of Vaso de Leche, held in Lima on October 25–26, 1986, the women from Villa El Salvador proposed that it be an autonomous organization, managed by committee women. All of the decision making had rested in Lima's city government during the first three years of the program.[10]

It's true that in Villa El Salvador, just as in the other metropolitan districts of Lima, the women had identified Vaso de Leche more with the city than with their own organization, the Women's Federation. Nevertheless, we believed that we knew all about the distribution of milk to children, and that we should be the ones to make decisions at the district level.

We took a management transfer proposal to Michel Azcueta, then mayor of Villa, and to the Urban Self-Management Committee of Villa El Salvador (CUAVES). Previously, we had not had success with CUAVES because the local directors tried to control everything. We had many arguments, but we insisted that we were the ones who actually made the program work.

The directorship of Vaso de Leche was transferred to the Women's Federation, to its 105 presidents of mothers' clubs, and to its 450 coordinators on March 8, 1987. We were vindicated. The mayor signed our by-laws. We pressured him by saying that we would demonstrate if he did not sign. Nobody believes in the capacity of women—that we can lead programs and be in charge of the administrative work. They imagine that we are going to make a mess of the receipts. In the beginning, even the women asked, "How are we going to do all this by ourselves?" And today there are sixty thousand who benefit from the program.

Vaso de Leche turned out to be an experience that provided federation women with opportunities to learn organizational and development skills while building self esteem. The women learned that they can resolve their own problems; they are in charge; they are capable.

After the transfer, we agreed to create eight supply centers, for a more effective distribution of the milk. We elected a subdirectorate to take responsibility for this task and to serve, at the same time, as an intermediate organizational unit in the federation. The women who work in each supply center decide their own agenda. Each supply center takes in fifteen to twenty residential groups. Each residential group has four Vaso de Leche committees.

The milk arrives each Thursday and is dispersed by the Villa municipality to the supply centers. But, not long ago, we agreed to pick up the milk from the municipality the same day that it arrived from Lima. The women from the federation, accompanied by a municipal worker, divided the milk among the supply centers, and from there the coordinators distributed it to the committees.

But what happened? We had another meeting in which we agreed that the Villa municipal worker should no longer go to Lima to get the milk. We signed an accord with the Villa government, and all of the jurisdiction was delegated to us. Now a social worker and member of the federation go to get the milk on a weekly basis. The municipality lets us use its truck. We even changed the appearance of the invoices. Whereas before they read "Municipality," now they read "Women's Federation." The Villa government intervenes only in legal matters pertaining to Lima.

Sure, this constant participation by the women signifies more than double or triple the work, but they take turns. Several residential groups are associated with each supply center; they take turns weekly. There is a certain amount of competition among the groups. If one group doesn't show up, it loses face. If the president can't go, her delegate, or even a recipient of the milk, can go. There are so many! There are between fifty and sixty mothers in each group.

Here, in Villa El Salvador, the transfer had a powerful impact on our women's organization. So we suggested that the city of Lima also turn over its program to the Lima Organizing Committee of Vaso de Leche and let it administer the entire program, which rightfully belongs to all the mothers.[11]

They have always said that the kitchens and the Vaso de Leche committees weaken the people and rob them of initiative. We say that this isn't so, because what we support is self-government. That is, we believe that people have to learn how to govern themselves. The poor have never governed the country; it has always been governed by an elite—a political elite. We contend that people can learn to govern themselves; they can learn from childhood onward, so that one day they will be capable of governing at the national level.[12]

5. With Gustavo Pineki, her husband. *La República*, from *María Elena Moyano: En busca de una esperanza.*

V

The Communal Kitchens

Because of hunger, unemployment, and misery, we created the communal kitchens.

We developed alternative solutions to alleviate the problems of hunger, unemployment, and the misery that we have been suffering. We created the kitchens because of this situation. They have already progressed through various stages and organizational structures.[13]

First, we organized ourselves so we could fill a common kettle and feed our children. Later, we wanted to achieve solidarity. So, as neighbors, we started to identify with each other's problems. For example, there was a mother who could not contribute her share to the common kettle, and we helped her. We also had to face the problem of getting along in our work. For example, we had to decide how to divide up the work on a rotating basis.

Once we faced the problem of how to respond to hunger, we also identified new goals. How were we going to organize, promote, and empower ourselves? Well, we did empower ourselves through the kitchens.

We have different kinds of kitchens in Villa El Salvador,[14] but those that have been most successful, or those that have been most replicated (like ants, we say, because one group begins a kitchen and others multiply), are the family kitchens. Twelve families organize them, and two families at a time take turns, putting in their work quota so they can eat during the rest of the week. And all of us take turns. We start by lending kettles, kitchens, and our utensils, and that's how we cook.

Each week we evaluate not only the quality of the food but also how we treat one another. That's how we identify other goals, because we don't just fill the kettle to fill it; we also deal with our problems, like rising costs, for example. In this way, we get better at organizing ourselves.

We have achieved much after so many years of organizing. But I believe that we must do more than stay in the kitchen to feed our children. If we just fill our children's stomachs, we will never get out of this crisis. We have many roads to travel; we have many rights to claim.

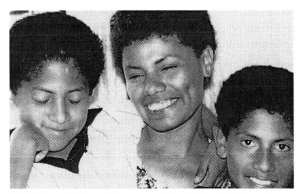

6. With her children, Gustavo and David. *La República,* from
María Elena Moyano: En busca de una esperanza.

VI

The Economic Crisis

Women have known how to respond to the economic crisis: Our
rights we demand, and handouts we remand.

The women's organizations have been set back the most by this crisis. The
poorest people, already impoverished by the shock politics of Belaúnde
[Fernando Belaúnde Terry] and Alán García [Alán García Pérez], organized survival programs like the communal kitchen and the Vaso de Leche
committees. Now others, somewhat better off than those described above,
have had to resort to similar tactics, given the brutal shock applied by the
Fujimori government in August 1990.

The people in these organizations, who admittedly don't represent the
majority of the public, urged the government to assist them, but the government added insult to injury and demanded that the communal kitchen
and the Vaso de Leche committees give up their rations instead. No won-
der the women in the organizations have felt frustrated.

New players are joining the struggle, like the municipalities, the neighborhood organizations, and the Church. But they don't know how to
confront the problem in a positive manner; they haven't recognized the
role played by the women who were organized even before the emergence
of shock politics. They don't realize that the women will not surrender

any more. There have been ongoing confrontations, not only in Villa El Salvador but also in the Lima metropolitan area. But women know how to deal with these problems. We also know how to resolve conflicts with the neighborhood organizations.

The Women's Federation has grown enormously, with its kitchens born out of the economic crisis and the monumentally damaging economic policies of August 1990. The organizations have had to increase rations to the maximum, and the members from the various Vaso de Leche committees have had to collaborate. They had to demonstrate on the streets to demand an increase in the Vaso de Leche allocation to bring attention to all of the families who need assistance.

I want to call upon the mothers who left Vaso de Leche because they didn't want to take their turns in the kitchens, participate in meetings or in demonstrations that their own organizations sponsored. These mothers left the program because their husbands worked, and they could afford to buy at least one carton of milk daily from ENCI (National Enterprise for the Marketing of Resources). Now these mothers no longer have that option. They must clamor for their milk. They must get involved like all the other mothers; they must take control, organize themselves into their respective committees, assume their responsibilities, and work for their rights.

Women have always known how to respond strongly to an economic crisis. They demand their rights, in the streets, if necessary, as the federation has done. We were the first to take to the streets to oppose "Fujishock." Our motto was "Shock for the rich and not for the poor! Rights we demand and handouts we remand!" We didn't want crumbs.

They spoke to us about an emergency plan that is directed at the poor. But seventy grams of fish and one hundred grams of rice do not solve the crisis. Instead, we proposed that the plan provide employment, so that male and female workers may eat with dignity. They applied their shock politics without really planning for the emergency.[15]

Decree 094 is being promulgated. Although the decree recognizes the roles of the metropolitan coordinating committees of Vaso de Leche and the national commission of the communal kitchens (in which the involvement of the Women's Federation is fundamental), that recognition is only on paper. They do not consider these organizations when making decisions. They turn all the money over to Caritas of Lima [Catholic Relief Services], which is very respectable, but we must ask the question: Why do our organizations exist in the first place? The members are the ones to whom the emergency programs should be turned over so that they can learn to direct them. In spite of all of their limitations, it should be the people in these organizations who learn how to deal with this crisis.

We do not think that the churches should be distributing the provisions. You can't educate the people this way because they don't learn how to govern themselves, to budget, or to audit. We don't like the idea that at any moment, every two or three days, the fiscal committee is visiting. This interference signifies a lack of trust in the people. We believe hungry people are also honest and resolved, and that they have demonstrated their honor and industriousness, as few have.

The Women's Federation and I, personally, do not like the way in which we are being audited, because frequently we are treated aggressively with shows of machismo and authoritarianism.

Through its Directorate of Communal Kitchens for the Southern Cone, the Women's Federation has signed an agreement with Care Perú by which the latter donates provisions directly to the supply centers.[16] I salute this development because it strengthens the popular movement. Women distribute the provisions; women do the auditing, conscious, of course, of their own norms and rules. Care Perú doesn't try to meddle or trip us up. It doesn't doubt the honesty of the mothers who work in the kitchens.

Women who previously did not belong to groups are now organizing themselves. They have asked to affiliate with the Women's Federation. The women from the mothers' clubs that received help from the Program for Direct Assistance (PAD), and who previously didn't want anything to do with the federation, will now have their reunion in Villa El Salvador.[17] The majority of them agreed to tightly coordinate their activities, and this is a big step forward. We are beginning to realize that when we organize, we come up with new approaches that enable us to defend our rights. Women are marginalized in this society, and this marginalization is expressed at all levels, even in the assistance programs.

In 1980 the women decided to organize themselves with the creation of the kitchens, the Vaso de Leche committees, and the mothers' clubs. They observed how, by organizing themselves, they contributed to the survival of their families. As a result, they realized the value of women's labor in the community. This awareness is of monumental importance because the Women's Federation carries on its shoulders the responsibility for feeding the people in this district, through its 1,500 Vaso de Leche committees and its 800 communal kitchens.

7. Beside a monument dedicated to the Women of Villa El Salvador. Photo by Victor Vargas, *Caretas*, from *María Elena Moyano, Perú en busca de una esperanza.*

VII

Local Government

In 1983 the people of Villa El Salvador succeeded in installing a local government in a community of over 300,000 inhabitants.

Making Villa El Salvador a municipality was the result of long years of struggle.[18] Michel Azcueta, of the United Left Party, a man much loved by our community, won the first election. Although he recognized women during his term, there were few women among the other elected officials. Those women who were elected did not reflect the concerns of the majority of women.

The same thing happened the second time around, when Michel Azcueta was reelected mayor. There was no woman who adequately represented the lives and the will of all of the organized women in Villa El Salvador. That is why, in an assembly of eight hundred delegates, the Women's Federation decided that we should participate in municipal politics.

At first there was much questioning. This type of response is not just characteristic of the women of Villa El Salvador, but of all Peruvian women. In fact, I think that this tendency pertains to the Peruvian people in general. They criticize attitudes, styles, and political decisions, from the most local to those of the national government. They question the authoritarianism of the political parties.

Women, by virtue of their willingness to question, know how democracy works because they have practiced it in their own organizations. They know what self-government means, and they practice it in all of their organizations.

In the latest elections, twenty of the political parties tried to get women to register on their rolls.[19] They were successful in capturing some who were the most active in the women's movement. Many women from Vaso de Leche and from the kitchens have served as aldermen. Even though these positions have limited influence, at least they are occupied by leaders who express the real thinking of the members of the women's organizations.

The participation of women in politics is a great achievement because these leaders, when elected as representatives of a political party, still represent the women's organizations and have their members' strong support, not only in all of the Lima area but also in the rest of the country.

Heretofore, the political parties did choose some women candidates. However, candidates who were chosen because they were women did not necessarily reflect the beliefs and concerns of the majority of women, nor did they possess an appreciation for their work.

Upon learning that the political parties were looking for members' support, the Women's Federation decided to hold an assembly to evaluate women's participation in local government. We decided to select a candidate who would run in our district's municipal elections. I had been president of the federation for two terms, and the *compañeras* decided that those women who had already fulfilled a significant role in the federation should run in the upcoming elections as delegates. Others ran for office in the elections held by the Urban Self-Management Committee of Villa El Salvador.

The federation chose me to be the candidate for the municipal elections. At the same time, the United Left, the political party with which I had been working, asked the Women's Federation if I could be their candidate. The federation accepted and supported the proposal. At first, we wondered what kind of support I would get if I ran for mayor of Villa El Salvador in the internal elections of the United Left. Given that, as a woman, I could not count on much support in this political organization if I ran for mayor, it was decided that I should run for deputy mayor. This is the position that I now enjoy, thanks to the cohesiveness of the women's vote and the support of others in my community.

I think it's significant to mention that women have not caused disputes within the political parties just because they've been asking questions. I think it's very important to labor within the parties as well as to work outside of them.

Returning to the theme of the municipalities: The women decided to hold personal campaigns for my candidacy. They made posters, signs, flyers, and organized folkloric events. They really made women's presence visible in the district. As a result of that campaign, few people knew the candidate for mayor, but many recognized me, the delegate whom the women had chosen to represent them in the municipal government.[20]

Just how did we win? First, we succeeded in getting the Women's Federation to administer Vaso de Leche. Second, we involved women who had previously not belonged to the Women's Federation. We also brought together the women's organizations that were sponsored by the state, like those mothers' clubs that began as a result of the initiative of one first lady or another in the President's Palace. During the past few administrations, each one had "her" own club in the newest *pueblo joven*. This support disappeared with any change of government.

We attracted a team of previously unorganized women to lead certain projects. In the case, for example, of the Support Program for Fair Wages (PAIT),[21] working mothers from our community asked the national government to pay them what they deserved, and they asked for the support of the Villa government. We went to the office of PAIT, occupied it, and prepared a communal kettle. The previously unorganized working women had not taken advantage of the federation because they did not feel part of it. They were used to going to the women's representative in the local government.

There is an industrial park in Villa El Salvador in which the owners of small and medium-sized businesses belong to an association. As a result of our participation in local government, we have been able to centralize all of the small businesses owned by women, so that they, too, may make their presence known in the industrial park.

The women also participated in health programs, in conjunction with other groups.[22] The health projects of the Women's Federation were incorporated within the overall activities sponsored by the municipality. We proposed that the municipal coordinators should not only concern themselves with solving general health problems, like environmental health and drug addiction, but also spearhead campaigns for women's health, including campaigns to diagnose vaginal infections—frequent in our district because of the scarcity of water—and campaigns to diagnose cervical cancer. As a result, we enjoyed the recognition and respect of all of the social forces: the Church, the Urban Self-Management Committee, and the neighborhood organizations.

The Women's Federation also worked to stem the tide of cholera.[23] We had to function on the periphery of the government's activities, however. The government would say, "You must boil your water for ten minutes." But this requires the consumption of a lot of fuel that we couldn't afford. Because we didn't have the fuel, at the onset of the epidemic, children drank unboiled water and became sick. Then we proposed that chlorine be used to purify barrels of water. Each *promotora* took the instructions to twenty-four women who represented the same number of families. Similarly, the government began a campaign against the consumption of fish. But for the poor families of Peru, fish is the most affordable food. We proposed that fish be eaten, but that it first be boiled or fried [not eaten raw as in seviche].

Because of machismo, one cannot always do as one would like within local government. Some lawmakers do not understand the role of women. We have to launch an intense and constant struggle with these lawmakers and with the mayor to make them respect the rights of organized women. We must do this not only to make them respect us but also to enable women to participate in each and every one of the decisions taken by the municipal government.

Lately, we have had to solve some problems regarding the ownership of land parcels. We have to find a way to resolve land ownership, given that some couples do separate. There is frequently a macho bias that must be addressed.

Even though there has been a significant increase in the number of female lawmakers, there is only one woman mayor—Mrs. Carabayllo. Our next goal is to increase our power in the municipal government, to place more women in Parliament, more in the Senate, as well as in the House of Representatives, and also—why not?—a woman in the executive office.

8. At the tenth anniversary celebration of the Flora Tristán Center for the Peruvian Woman, 1989. Photo by Juan Guerra, from *María Elena Moyano, Perú en busca de una esperanza*.

VIII

The Women's Committees for the Protection of the Consumer

> The monitors are leaders in their own communities, working to prevent fiscal abuses, providing guidelines for the seller and the consumer.

We confronted a new challenge with the Women's Committees for the Protection of the Consumer.[24] We women are effective protagonists when we participate in the decision making of the local government.

For example, garbage is a serious problem. We explain to the women that there must be clean-up campaigns because there are too few municipal trucks and workers to do the job. Then, in a massive movement, as though they were ants, the women clean up the community. Just as they clean their own houses, they clean the whole district of Villa El Salvador.

Now we have a new endeavor—the Women's Committees for the Protection of the Consumer and the People's Tranquility, composed of delegates who are elected in the meetings of the Vaso de Leche committees or in the communal kitchen meetings. The municipality provides training in environmental health, sanitary inspection, price control, drug addiction, domestic violence, and the rights of women. We want these women to become teachers. We also want them to monitor the safety and tranquility of our community and to protect the consumer.

We have serious problems with the street vendors and merchants, even though we have good communication with them. According to statistics, the majority of vendors in Peru are women. In spite of the fact that we monitor them, we can't deny the fact that some of the weights they use are faulty, permitting them to rob one hundred or two hundred grams for each kilo of rice or sugar they sell. Others alter some prices. They hold back food or try to corner the market when there are shortages of some staples. We maintain cordial relationships with them, while we work as a team with the community economic monitors.

The monitors visit the markets, stores, and bodegas to verify that fair prices are being charged. They also check the hygiene at the places selling food. Because we have serious water supply problems, this effort is a priority in Villa El Salvador. It is essential that each volunteer exert every possible effort to reduce the health problems in our community.

Recently, a number of *salsódromos* [places where young people dance to salsa music] have opened. We have good relations with the youth; we should not close the places where they have fun, but these places should be monitored to prevent altercations. The monitors check to see that the hours during which the fiestas occur coincide with community regulations.

The monitors also watch out for the sale of drugs. The selling of drugs is illegal in our country, and we see, with great alarm, that many drugs are being sold to the young in our community. So these women take on this task, each becoming a kind of municipal policewoman. The municipality has trained them and has empowered them to work freely in this capacity.

This practice is new, untried; it doesn't exist in any other part of Peru. The municipal police, who are mostly men, wear uniforms and carry a badge. They aren't up on the prices when they monitor the markets. Women, on the other hand, are always aware of any price changes because their families' health and lives depend on this information. They are also concerned with the safety of their neighborhoods; they worry about their own and their neighbors' children and want to know what they are doing in the barrio.

All of this new participation by women is very significant. Here, they are not just dealing with survival issues. Their involvement in the community has had a great impact. The interest of the local government has been aroused because part of our community's problems, and much of the criticism lodged against local government, have been caused by its failure to control prices and improve hygiene in the markets. Some of the economic problems in our community, such as market cornering and speculation, have been alleviated by this group of one hundred women, who have also succeeded in diminishing the disorder in our community.

9. With King Juan Carlos of Spain, 1990. From *María Elena Moyano, Perú en busca de una esperanza.*

IX

The Terror of the Shining Path

> I could never destroy what I have built with my own hands.

A year ago, *El Diario* attacked me and the Women's Federation.[25] It said that we serve as a mattress for the system, and that we neither elevate nor value women because women will only be emancipated through war. It said that we are assisting the government, and that I am a "revisionist" who manipulates women. It took and published photos of the Women's House.[26] Sendero is an ongoing threat. It seems to me that its first objective has been to disparage the Women's Federation in order to deal it a blow later.

For a long time, I thought Sendero was a group that, although mistaken, was, in some way, fighting for justice. But I totally rejected it when Senderistas killed labor leader Enrique Castilla.[27] Previously, I didn't dare condemn the terrorist tactics used by Sendero. Now, however, it is attacking the organizations of the poor. Why? Who are the people in Vaso de Leche? Those who can't afford to eat in their own homes. I don't understand this group of unstable people.[28] Are they not undermining our organizations and increasing the levels of malnutrition and death?

If it had wanted, the left could have tried to change the scene. It was the only force capable of defeating Sendero in this country. People didn't agree with the strategies of the right. The only alternative was the left, at least before it became divided.

The left had been in touch with the people who were the most needy, the most dispossessed. Sendero has advanced by terrorizing the left. Many *compañeros* deserted because they felt betrayed and disillusioned and found no other option.

Some people in the barrios look at Sendero from a distance. They see it as something mythical. The Senderistas say they fight for equality. I think the left has a grave responsibility. The Senderistas gave up on what remained of the left. The most radical among them wanted to carve out their own territory. Now, who from the left has come forward to denounce the bombing in Villa? No one. Has any political leader come forward to see what is happening with the organizations, to learn how the mothers are, or if they want to continue working in the kitchens?

I don't know what they're trying to do with their parliamentary commissions and their clowning around. The people laugh at their methods. They just aren't doing enough. We need to fortify the community organizations.

If I have courage, it is because the women of the federation have given it to me. We met on the very day that Sendero placed the bomb in our center. We reacted rapidly. The women gave me strength and valor when they agreed to repudiate Sendero. The metropolitan assembly of communal kitchens also agreed to mobilize, taking the example of Villa El Salvador and using the watchwords "Against hunger and terror."

There were no cohesive organizations in Ayacucho. Puno's organizations were strong, but there was a political problem. The United Mariátegui Party (PUM)[29] divided and left an opening for Sendero to enter. It is very difficult to penetrate cohesive organizations.

On one hand, we have had the economic crisis, and on the other, the dispersion of the vanguard. Take, for example, the divisive problems that existed in the Urban Self-Management Committee and which, happily, have been overcome. Also, each faction within the left wanted to have hegemony. The country needs the unification of the left.

The Senderistas are mistaken if they think the kitchens are going to close. Where is a mother going to feed her family if not there? For this reason, when I hear these rumors, I say it is impossible for the kitchens to close. Those who do not eat there die of hunger. We must dispel the fear.

The women are very strong. We believe in what we are building; there is no need to fear. We are working for the well-being of the people, for solidarity and justice. It would be better to challenge Sendero. I have done it. I told the Senderistas that many people are ready to join in the fight for development and justice, but without the terror and assassinations. I no longer believe that Sendero is a revolutionary group. It has become a terrorist group.

On the other hand, the people don't have any confidence in the police force of this country. The police practice violence and often murder people. They would have to do much to gain the confidence of the people. Let them bring about justice with the disappeared, tortured, imprisoned, and assassinated.[30] Then we could have faith in their desire for order.

The defeat of Sendero has to be both political and ideological. It wages more than a military struggle. A new approach must emerge to counter Sendero's political agenda. That is why I say the forces of the left must get involved. Before the left divided, Barrantes [Alfonso Barrantes Lingán], [Javier] Diez Canseco, and [Manuel] Dammert came to see us.[31] The three treated us badly. The left divided, and now you have the consequences. The country needs unity.

The community organizations and the unions must create security mechanisms. They should agree to defeat the terror. The directors of the kitchens and of Vaso de Leche, for example, have united behind one objective: to defend what they have built. I believe that women are very courageous. Additionally, the organizations can bring in new leadership. Sure, not all of the barrios are organized, but this is all we have, and it is the most effective approach. We must continue to combat Sendero, rejecting its terrorist acts.

Sendero has murdered peasants and popular leaders. I believe that assassination has become a way of life for the Senderistas. It is their tactic, as they call it. And they will continue. They have to assassinate our leaders in order to control Lima.

There are people who ask if I am afraid. Yes, at times I am, but I am very firm and have moral strength. I have always been ready to surrender my life. I have faith. Something may change if the women respond in Lima. We can defeat Sendero if the people organize and centralize their forces. The situation is not easy, but it is also not impossible.

Letter of Reply to Sendero Luminoso from María Elena Moyano, Regarding Its Defamation of Her Character

To the political parties that are aware of their obligations to our country
To my neighbors in Villa El Salvador and the people's organizations
To the Urban Self-Management Committee
To the women of Villa El Salvador[32]

With great indignation, I received a flyer that has been circulating and bears the initials "MCB" [Barrio Class Movement].[33] It justifies the Communist Party of Peru [Sendero Luminoso] and lodges a series of calumnies against me. I feel an urgent need, in the face of this denunciation, to state the following:

1. They accuse me of being allied with the government and with the armed forces. You are witnesses to the fact that, even as a young leader, and as president of the Women's Federation, I always fought against governments that oppressed the people. I also denounced the human rights violations (genocide in the prisons, searches, paramilitary groups). Under my direction, the federation was the only organization in Villa El Salvador that brought together thousands of women to protest Fujishock and Change 90.[34]

2. They accuse me of trying to form urban patrols in conjunction with the armed forces. You, who have known my history in Villa El Salvador for the past twenty years, could never believe this. I oppose the army's intrusion. The patrols have been a part of Villa El Salvador's history. Since their establishment, they have functioned as autonomous neighborhood units to deal with delinquency and drug addiction.

3. They accuse me of robbing the people. You know that, since the age of fifteen, I have worked to promote early education, literacy, and health. I did all of this work on a voluntary basis. The mothers whom I taught to read and write, and the children, who are now youths, are proof.

Since the creation of the Women's Federation, you have seen me, walking the sandy streets of Villa El Salvador, working to develop its infrastructure.

I surrendered to my work and sacrificed without receiving anything in exchange.

Let me make something clear: In regard to the money from Canada, they say they have a thousand eyes. If that's true, how come they can't see the four equipped supply centers? Look at them! I already explained I would never administer that money—not as an individual, nor as a director. It was administered by the Canadian institution.

In regard to the money from ISIS [one of the first feminist groups with a global perspective], they say they have a thousand ears. Then why don't they listen to the proceedings of the coordinating committee meetings? The commission responsible for administering the money provided detailed information on its distribution of working capital to the federation's four supply centers and its use for the purchase of a generator and a large scale. The federation will confirm this information.

In regard to the milk: Never in my leadership history have I distributed milk or any other food. My role as president didn't require it. There were always committees that did it. The committee responsible for provisioning buys from the district committee, with its own money, and then sells the provisions to the kitchens. The federation can verify this.

In regard to the fines on businesses: If they have a thousand ears, they will hear the people clamor for controls and for sanctions to be imposed on some businesses. The women monitors do this, but the money received goes to the municipality and later serves the people.

4. They accuse me of dynamiting the supply center and say "it was not them." Let's take a look at my history: Since its earliest days, I have contributed to the development of the federation. My custom is to build. Since the time I was twelve years old, I helped my mother build community centers, medical posts, nonformal, early education programs, tree planting programs, etc. As a teenager, I formed youth groups like "Community's Children" and "Renew." I helped with the formation of the Committee for Promoters of Early Education and served as its president. As a mother, I began women's and mothers' clubs, hundreds of kitchens and Vaso de Leche committees. As president, I helped to develop all of the local centers that today belong to the federation (supply centers and the Women's House).

I could never destroy what I have built with my own hands. My actions speak for me. Radical discourse and calumny can't change that. I am thankful for the solidarity of organized women, for the support of the youth of Villa El Salvador, and for my neighbors, who saw me grow up during Villa El Salvador's twenty-year history.

Finally, neighbors, the revolution is an affirmation of life and of individual and collective dignity. It is our ethic. Revolution is not death, nor imposition, nor submission, nor fanaticism. Revolution is new life—the belief in and struggle for a just and dignified society—in support of the organizations the people have created, respecting their internal democracies, sowing new seeds of power in a new Peru. I will continue to stand with my people, with the women, youth, and children; I will continue to fight for peace with social justice.

Viva Life

María Elena Moyano,

Former President, the Women's Federation of FEPOMUVES

10. With Diana Miloslavich Tupac, February 9, 1992, at La Punta beach, port of Callao. From Diana Miloslavich Túpac.

X

On the Side of Life

> I believe it is very difficult to defeat, with fear and terror, what people have built with their own hands, strength, and spirit.

This is what we say to the *compañeras* in the local organizations. And this spirit has been demonstrated by the women of Villa El Salvador. Terror must be defeated—the fear that can be sown among us. Here is our example of how to defuse this fear. On the twenty-sixth [September 26, 1991], the workers in all of the kitchens in the Lima metropolitan area are going to demonstrate, using the example of the women of Villa El Salvador. They are going to march in the streets. Marches have been a traditional form of protest for the people, a way to learn and to teach.

We are marching to protest terrorist acts of intimidation, like the assassination of our leaders. The terrorists are threatening our organizations, and when they touch the people and what the people have built, the people will fight. The people will defend what they have built. I don't think this will happen, however. Organized women in this country have learned to stand up for what they believe in, and now they are doing it in a significant way.

I want to explain that the people haven't reacted until now because they lacked faith [in their institutions]. So many human rights have been violated! Our young people have been murdered; they have been made to disappear. There's the case of the disappearance of the young student in Villa El Salvador.[35] So where are the people going to turn if there is no confidence in this government or in its military forces?

The political parties, without exception, are in total disrepute; the people do not think well of them. In these circumstances, it is the people who must confront Sendero. The first defeat must be a political one. I don't think that there should be a military confrontation. I don't have guns or the arms to challenge Sendero. I believe that there has to be a contest of goals. Sendero has a political agenda for the country, with a strategy and all. We, too, have to come up with our proposal. What is it we want for this country? What is it we want to build?

The country has not yet realized that it's the women's organizations that deal with survival issues and the neighborhood organizations that we've built, with our hands and efforts, that offer the direction for the new Peru, assuming, of course, that the government does its part.

How can we say that we're going to defeat Sendero if, at the same time, the government denies its support to the thousands of survival organizations that help people endure this country's crisis? What has the government given these organizations that help people meet their basic needs? Is there legislation to support the kitchens?[36] The legislation is useless. Is there a budget?

This country's government, political parties, and representatives don't recognize just how much they are damaging what the people, who have lost faith in the political parties, have built. The people have organized and created their own defense mechanisms. Of course, the people are not going to approve of terrorist acts because they are the ones who suffer.

We have responded to Sendero, telling the Senderistas they are mistaken if they think they can change the country in their manner. You don't change a country through the assassination of popular leaders, by attacking the people's organizations, and by killing even the priests who work with the people. To those who think that Sendero is fighting for the country, we reply that it will not be its members who move this country ahead; it will be the people who learn to take charge of their own destinies.

The Senderistas are killing our directors. Today we learned that they killed a director of Vaso de Leche in Callao. Are they only killing police? Are they only killing mayors? Are they only killing congressmen? Today they are killing mothers with families. The general public does not react because Sendero has not yet touched them. But today they touched us, and we must unite with an organized and strong response. We know how to do this. We must very carefully state, to this terrorist group, that it is the Senderistas who oppose the people. Until now, many of the women directors have said, "Yes, they are *compañeros* who fight for the people." Not any longer. False. They fight against the people. They are opposed to our organizations.

We align ourselves with life. Let those with political proposals present them so they may be discussed and debated. Sendero must not threaten our directors, because if it touches just one *compañera* or one director in Villa El Salvador, the people of Villa will rise up. We are not afraid of anyone, and we're prepared to give our lives.

Letter to Emma Hilario[37]

Emma:

I learned of the attempt on your life, after having returned from a trip. I want to tell you that an attempt to kill you is an attempt to kill the poorest and neediest people. There is no name for what they have done. Nothing remains to us except the efforts of an organized people and the consciousness of the women of our towns. I do not tell you to be careful because many people tell us that, and, in the end, nobody takes care of us or supports us. All that remains, Emma, is the fortitude that comes from the hearts of our oppressed people. The terror will only be defeated with that force.

Your compañera,

María Elena Moyano

January 1992

11. "For a Life with Hope in a Land of Peace. María Elena Lives among Us." *La República,* March 8, 1992.

XI

The People's Movement

Twenty thousand women demonstrated against hunger and terror.[38]

We are suffering economic conditions that are the product of neoliberal politics that oppress and crush the poorest people. Furthermore, the military forces are violating human rights. We cannot forget the thousands of dead. There is also the terrorist group that annihilates the leaders of our people and threatens to impose its terror on all of our country. Today it threatens the communal kitchens, where it finds the poorest people.

In light of these circumstances, we propose that the government change the political and economic situation by taking the following steps: raising salaries; providing equity in taxation; supporting nutrition legislation; and fortifying peasants by giving them machinery and seeds, instead of arms, to combat Sendero.

In contrast to the group that says we should "fight for justice," we propose that the people should govern themselves. We believe in the organizations the people, out of necessity, have generated to deal with the economic situation. And we believe in the people's right of self-defense.

We are convinced that this oppressive situation must change so that the needy have opportunities in all areas—health, education, and also in politics, where the elite have dominated, and the people have not participated.

This change will be achieved through the support supplied by the local organizations and through popular democracy, autonomy, and justice. I don't think the armed forces should deliver food in the barrios, and they shouldn't have a presence there. We don't have confidence in them. There would be indignation. It is too late.

We propose that there be an accord that arises from the coordinated efforts of the people, orchestrated by an entity previously known as the National Popular Assembly (ANP).[39] This assembly would include all of the organizations and would represent the poorest people. This accord must have two fundamental tenets: it must be against hunger; it must be against terror.

The people must democratically decide when to use the mechanism of self-defense, without having it imposed upon them. They must take a position and decide how to defend themselves.

In addition to bearing the effects of the government's crushing economic policies that have worsened the already exhausted condition of our people, the people now suffer attacks from the Senderistas, who are programmed to destroy our organizations and, through threats and terror, to end neighborhood leadership.

It is clear that Sendero Luminoso is concentrating its efforts in Lima and, particularly, in the barrios, in accordance with its plan geared at achieving "strategic equilibrium." But in order for it to advance, it must do away with the Vaso de Leche committees, the communal kitchens, and the various survival and neighborhood organizations. This is a task it will not accomplish, because the women of the barrios want peace for the country, and they reject terrorism, as seen at the mass demonstration of September 26.

They killed Juana López León, a Vaso de Leche director.[40] They tried to destroy one of the supply centers of the Women's Federation of Villa El Salvador. However, the women, who have worked in the communal kitchens since 1978, and in Vaso de Leche since 1984, are standing firm, providng an example, teaching how to construct democracy from the bottom up, demonstrating that they can survive and still generate new jobs, thus contributing to national development and to social transformation.

These are the women who demand that the government pay attention to Law 25307 in its national budget. This law recognizes the grassroots organizations and creates a support program for their current nutritional work. Day after day, the women in these organizations demonstrate their management skills. These are the women who forge unity; they know that by being united, they will provide for their children's well-being.

In the immediate future, it is essential to generate a wide citizen mobilization that results, for example, in district accords that favor peace and democracy and unite those of us who stand for life and not for war and death. Unity will help us overcome our fears. Additionally, as a means of protecting the grassroots organizations, and as an affirmation of democracy, we should use the neighborhood patrols for our own defense in everyday life.

Part Two

Autobiography

I spent the best days of my life in Villa El Salvador.

My name is María Elena Moyano Delgado. I was born on November 29, 1958, in the Barranco District of Lima. My parents were Eugenia Delgado Cabrera and Hermógenes Moyano Lescano. I have six brothers and sisters: Rodolfo, Raúl, Carlos, Narda, Eduardo, and Martha. I am married and have two children, I am busy with my family and my organization. I live in Sector 3, Group 18, Lot 15. I studied two years of sociology at the university level.

I have happy memories of my father and family, at least until I reached the age of five. We lived in Surco, in a house near the park and my school. The best part of my childhood was having my parents together and my time in school. I could read and write at an early age. I attended the little school on the park. I remember that my teacher's name was René. Later I attended a state-run primary school. My teacher was named Asunción; she was very good. I never did receive a diploma. Well, I was very active, unlike my brothers, who were glued to the books. But I never repeated a school year. I was one of a group of children that was always making mischief.

I felt useless when I lived in Barranco and Surco, although I admit it was also frustrating moving to a desert. [Villa El Salvador lies on a barren coastal strip.] I remember that first day when we were dropped off with our things. There was my mother and my brothers and sisters. My siblings were a little older than I, and they fought to see who would go to buy the straw mats and poles. My sister [Narda] and I were very afraid.

By evening, we finished making a basic shack. Four mats made a square room, with one on top for the roof. I remember there was a lot of wind, and that the roof almost blew off at night. Everything was dark, and all you could hear was the whistle of the wind. We didn't even have a candle.

My sister and I couldn't sleep all night. I joined my brothers and sisters in telling my mother that the situation was horrible. We said, "And now what do we do?" But my mother thought that here, at least, nobody would throw us out of this shack, and that here, one day, we would build our home. She told us where the bathroom would be, the living room, the bedroom. She said that each of us would have our own bedroom, and if the lot wasn't large enough, we would make a spiral staircase and have more bedrooms on the second floor.

I remember when they threw us out of our house and seized our furniture. That experience gave us even more desire to endure and more dreams for our own pretty house with a little living room, kitchen, bath, and bedrooms. I wouldn't need a patio. We would have a huge one; it would be the central park in which, one day, there would also be a place for us to gather and play volleyball.

Those first months we all worked hard to finish our house of straw mats and poles. We eventually added several rooms.

Later I got involved in the church. We formed a youth group and prepared a theatrical production for Holy Week about the passion and death of our Lord, Jesus Christ. Once, I played the role of Mary Magdalene. These events took place on Sundays. On weekdays, I traveled to a school in Surco called Jorge Chávez. I left with my brother at five in the morning to get in line to take bus number 55, which dropped us at the stop near Higuereta. From there, we walked about a half hour. We were on the school's volleyball team, and so we had to return to school in the afternoons to train.

I also remember that we were hungry a lot. My brothers and sisters didn't work, and my mother couldn't find clothes to wash. Nevertheless, we always returned home for lunch. To my mother, everything that had to do with school came first. At times we lied, saying that we had classes in the afternoon, knowing she would give us bus money so we could go to volleyball practice. During the summers, I would play volleyball in the Villa championships.

I spent my days at the secondary school or at church.

At age fifteen I finished secondary school at Jorge Chávez in Surco. My brothers wanted Narda and me to apply to the university. A school friend and I wanted to enroll in a secretarial program instead. There was an extension course offered by the University of Lima. When the time came, I asked my brothers if it could be my sister who applied to the university because, otherwise, there would not be enough money for the two of us. I reminded them that I preferred a practical career. My sister applied to the University of San Marcos; I did not. She was not admitted.

Later, the entrance exams for the Garcilaso de la Vega University came up. My brother Carlos asked us to apply, but we didn't want to. He promised to work for us and said that he would pay our fees. We agreed and applied together. I added the condition that I be allowed to choose my own career. My mother opposed this arrangement. She wanted me to study law. I lied to her, saying that, yes, I would, but instead I applied to the sociology program. Anyway, I thought that I'd never be accepted. Unlike my sister, I had never been educated in an academy; I only wanted to read books about different societies. Unfortunately, I was admitted.

When the exam results were released, I was already in love with Gustavo, who is now my husband. I didn't want to go to the university, but he insisted. I went with my fiancé, and my sister went with hers. The first thing I did was look at the acceptance list for the accounting program, the career track that my sister had chosen, but her name was not on the list. "Well," I told Gustavo, "this university is off limits for the poor," and I angrily commented that we should not have wasted time or money in applying, least of all at a private university. This was my brothers' madness. And we had even lied, saying we lived in Barranco, and had also put on the personal data sheet that we had a very wealthy father, who was a businessman, and a number of other things, and still we were not admitted. I thought I was right to think one had to have a lot of money to get into that university.

My sweetheart then insisted that we look at the sociology list. I was very surprised to see my name on it. I couldn't believe it. I was sad because I couldn't understand why they had not admitted my sister, who was more studious and better prepared than I, and who now would not have the same chances in life. I didn't say anything at home for one week. I was so sad, but I finally had to tell my brother.

I became director of a musical theater group shortly after entering the university.[1]

There were fifty young people from different neighborhoods who, independently of the Church, gathered in the local hall. It was a beautiful group. I remember each one of them, the activities we had, and how we reflected on the Bible, the problems of the young, drugs, and the lack of communication with our parents.

We were just young people, with Christian convictions, who were loyal to our community. There was no adult to guide or influence us. We were youths with a desire to do something for our community. We helped the directors and sang and performed before large meetings, where neighbors would debate the issues. We developed our own themes. I must say that we did not see the people from the Popular Communication Center. We thought they would try to manipulate us politically. We were always careful around them, and we competed with them when we learned they would be performing in one of the neighborhoods; we polished our acts and rehearsed to leave a good impression of our group.

I can't forget the time there was a youth conference, and we were invited. I remember Yoni,[2] who told me that the Bible wasn't sufficient to end the problems of young people. I argued with him, trying to convince him and the others that what was important was love of our neighbor; that if we could just be good and united, it would be enough.

I studied historical and dialectical materialism at the university—class struggle, et cetera. Then I began to question myself. I didn't understand why so many of the poor had to struggle so hard to study or to get work. They couldn't succeed. What was our problem? Incapacity? What? I asked myself many questions, and finally I began to question the existence of God, and, if He existed, why did He allow so many children to die from hunger, and why were there so many frustrated young people?

About the same time, some university students approached our youth group. They promised to help us with the theater, to write the scripts, to train our voices, et cetera. At first, they tried to teach us something, but they were very boring. We had our own way of thinking, our own music, and our own way of dancing. Later, we turned off the music, and we shared our problems or accounts of something that had mortified us, and we helped each other; we would reflect on a problem together. They [on the other hand] wanted to teach us the thesis of Mao, who spoke of the obligations of the individual, but the lessons were boring, and they turned off the students. Very few of us remained with them.

They [the university students] began a class to teach us about Marxism and about the Chinese revolution. We talked about class struggle. I, who had only a minimal amount of university instruction, and they, who were much older, spoke about the same things. They said that the Church was the opiate of the people. A point came when I no longer believed in God. Only a few remained from our original group, and all of us were leaders. Now, I very much regret not having been able to help some of the other students, younger than we, who are now marginalized. They still respect us, however, and have never harmed us. On the contrary, they have always been supportive.

The directors decided there was a need for a school for the young children of the members of our circle. The school had to belong to the people and not to the state. They asked all of the young women who had finished their secondary educations, and who wanted to care for children aged three to five years, to come forward at the next meeting because they would select someone to be in charge. I was chosen, and they asked me to prepare myself for the task.[3] It was exciting for me to become a teacher that easily.

I began to work with a group of children in the mornings. I remember that we had very little. The children sat on stones or bricks. One day my fiancé, Gustavo, brought some wood and made a table for us. He shaped it into a circle, and the children had a place to draw and paint. I dreamed about an ideal, early childhood education facility, about the kind the directors talked about doing with the help of UNICEF. I dreamed about having a bathroom and a real classroom for the children. I worked for four years in the local community center while the module was being constructed. I never had the chance to teach there, but my youngest son attended that facility.

I worked alone at the first PRONOEI [nonformal, experimental] early childhood program in Villa El Salvador.

The following year, more educational programs began in Villa El Salvador. I was chosen to be the specialist in charge of educational evaluation. The teachers got together so that the instructional coordinator could train us, but we were unsuccessful when we tried to apply the information. We had neither the materials nor the kind of children they had in Miraflores [a much wealthier Lima neighborhood]. So we formed the Study Circle for Nonformal Teachers (CEA). We taught ourselves the instructional methodology and the curriculum used by the Ministry of Education.

We never thought of a salary until more coordinators arrived. We learned that some of them were not specialists, did not have experience but were, nevertheless, earning salaries. Then, through our study circle, we asked the Community Education Nucleus (NEC) to keep our own promoters in mind—those who had experience and some training—when they contracted for future coordinators.

The year that the Education Workers of Peru (SUTEP) struck, the union leaders came to our circle and asked us for our support, telling us that we, too, had grievances, and that the state should be responsible for the education of the children by paying teachers. They told us that we were teachers, uncredentialed, but teachers. The educational leaders of the Urban Self-Management Committee also supported the strike. All of the parents did, too. So we decided to form a committee of strikers from Villa El Salvador. We asked for a minimum salary and the right to be coordinators. The community decided to form the Central Strike Committee, composed of a member from the Urban Self-Management Committee, one from the Education Workers of Peru group, a parent, and a representative from the education promoters. I was elected as the representative from Villa El Salvador. As a show of strength, the committee agreed to occupy the schools, demonstrate, and throw paint on the yellows [scabs].

They assign me to a school.

The Central Strike Committee delegated responsibility for the occupation of the schools. I was assigned to a school. I had no experience, but I still participated with great conviction and a sense of mythical proportion. I was convinced that only societal change could end the injustice against the people. I remember when the Pachacútec school was occupied—the school that turned out to be the model. It was considered the strongest school because the educational nucleus was there. I remember the woman who became famous as Comandante Zero. She was a mother with children in the school. I spent my first night away from home in that school. My mother was desperate, thinking that something had happened to me. Well, tanks did come. I don't remember how they entered because there was so much sand.

That stage in my life really changed me. I did not live at home; I lived at the "Pacha" school. I left my family; I had a different family during the entire strike. My mother was Comandante Zero, and the teachers, students, and promoters were my brothers and sisters. It was our home. I remember how we rotated tasks, in such a disciplined way, and with a feeling we were involved in a spiritual revolution. The occupation was disciplined, especially during the night watches. I didn't sleep one moment the first night. Every time I saw a car pass, I blew a whistle that made everyone jump out of their beds and leave through the windows. I didn't let anyone sleep. They never assigned me to that watch again.

It was such an emotional time! I remember how we would go out early in the morning to gather food at the markets and the solidarity of the people. It was so beautiful! What unity! I remember how we walked from school to school as though it were nothing. Everyday the people would prepare communal kettles. I'll never forget the famous soups, so delicious: sweet potato, cauliflower, yucca, *olluco,* and all of the vegetables that would be donated, prepared with great gusto by Comandante Zero and "Fat Alfred."

I also remember when the *apros* [members of APRA, the American Popular Revolutionary Alliance][4] removed the parents from "school occupation number five," Public School 6065. All of the Central Strike Committee prepared to retake "five." All of the families gathered and planned, minute by minute, how we would recapture the school and throw out the *apros.* It was said that they had guns and knives. We got clubs. I was responsible for getting the self-defense weapons. Although I was very afraid, I accepted this duty. I can't forget a *compañero* who was bleeding profusely from a head injury. We were even told that one of us could die; that we should take care of each other. That day I gathered stones for the *compañeros* who had to oust the yellows. I remember the mobilizations, the tear gas, and the clubs.

I believed we were engaging in revolution.

I must say that even though I had a revolutionary consciousness, I knew nothing about political parties. I knew only that APRA was opposed to our cause.

It was my experience that the education promoters who did not actively participate in the strike, were not invited to the meetings. I believed that it was our cause, and that we had to fight for it together. I understood that not everyone was in favor of the strike. Some of the nonformal teachers even replaced the regular teachers during the long strike, although we really wouldn't let anyone work. Ms. Vilcachagua had a list of the yellows who were "working."

To pay my university fees, I substituted for teachers on maternity leave.

I forgot to mention that, to earn money to pay my university fees, I substituted for teachers who were on maternity leave. During the strike, I taught at Public School 6063 in the mornings and at one PRONOEI school in the afternoons. I also remember that although Ms. Vilcachagua knew I was coordinator of the preschool, nonformal teachers, she offered me a contract and even guaranteed me a position in a school. She tried to convince me that those who initiated the strike were politicians. I rejected the offer. Of course, I couldn't return to any school once the strike ended. But I had the satisfaction of knowing that Vilcachagua promised there would be no retaliation against the directors and nonformal teachers once the strike ended, on the condition that I not return to teach at any PRONOEI school. I remember how all the *compañeras* turned their backs on Vilcachagua and unanimously agreed to continue with the strike if she did not allow me to return. She had no other recourse, and I was able to finish the year at my PRONOEI school.

Later, I didn't have any work, and my mother was pressuring me because I wasn't helping out at home. I couldn't substitute-teach anymore because of my strike involvement, and so I couldn't pay for the academic term. I also learned that the political parties took advantage of each school occupation. Some teachers were even inviting me to insider meetings. So, with all the pressure from my family, with hundreds of teachers replaced, with some *compañeros* in prison, I felt frustrated, as if I had accomplished nothing. My only consolation was my ever-patient fiancé. We had been together for five years, and my mother adored him—the ideal son-in-law.

I decided to surrender to him and to have a baby. I had wanted to have one. I didn't understand it, but I wanted to raise, educate, and give my child everything that I could not have: a family with an exemplary father. I got pregnant. I didn't want to get married and didn't even want Gustavo to be responsible for supporting the baby. Gustavo had his own economic problems. He was the oldest of seven orphaned brothers and sisters, and his father was in prison. He also had a pregnant sister to take care of. An entire family for which he was responsible. I would have been too much.

I looked for work but couldn't find any, and, to top it off, the pregnancy caused me to become very anemic—a product of the communal kettles and my bad kidneys. I couldn't sleep at night. My brothers learned that I was pregnant. My pregnancy created total chaos in the family. My mother cried and shamed me. She scolded me, saying that if she couldn't get married in white, her daughter should. My brothers wanted to kill me. While I was ill and at home, my youngest brother psychologically abused me. No one forgave me for losing my job and leaving the university for some strike that produced no visible gains. They threw it in my face that I had been used by the politicians. While I was in bed, they would ask me, "Where are your friends now that you are going to have a child?"

My mother speaks to Gustavo and asks him to marry me.

Gustavo was, of course, delighted. He had already told me that in spite of all the economic difficulties, we would get married. I believed that marriage was not the solution to any problem, least of all the problem of having a baby. But I remembered how I had suffered when I was a little girl, when my parents separated, without a father at my side, and the oft-repeated words of my mother, "Since I didn't have luck in marriage, and did not have the good fortune to get married in white, you, my daughters, will certainly leave this house in white."

My mother arranged all the details of the civil and religious ceremonies.⁵ She paid the expenses. My oldest brother rented the bridal dress; my youngest brother, Eduardo, gave us the cake and the appetizers; my sister-in-law, Beatriz, and my other brothers and sisters provided the food and beer. My mother did the invitations, and I got married just as my mother had dreamed of getting married herself: in the Barranco church, where I had also been baptized, with a white gown and a train, three bridesmaids, two nephews carrying my train, and one niece bearing the rings. As I entered the church, I thought only of the young people in the strike and remembered the struggle. I could see my *compañeros* Miguel and Josefina. I felt sad. Was I beginning a new life only to leave my people's revolutionary struggle? On the other hand, I dreamed of the ideal family and awaited the birth of my child.

I begin a new life.

I had problems in creating the ideal family—my new goal. I lived in a room made of straw mats that belonged to my mother. My brothers were not working. I was sick because of the pregnancy. My husband had another family to support. We lived on the little that my *compañero* earned, and he also helped to feed my brothers. I remember that my brother Carlos, who had children, was also jobless. My sister Narda was the only one working. I remember the fights, the absolute subordination to my husband. I cooked for him, but he did not like the taste of the food I prepared, and so I cried. I did not eat so I could save the best for him. I didn't want him to ever reproach me by saying that he supported my family.

I remember the birth of my child in those poor circumstances. I used the little money that Gustavo gave me for diapers and maternity fees for food.

The day my pains began, my mother looked for Felícita, the health worker. She checked me and said I was not yet ready. My mother and husband decided to wait a little longer so the maternity hospital would not send me back home. At 7:00 P.M. on August 2, 1980, my son was born in my mother's bed. I was attended by my husband and Señora Felícita. My husband held his son at birth. It was a marvelous experience. My child, so longed for.

I lived with my mother. Gustavo also had to support his own family. His sister had a child, but her *compañero* did not assume responsibility. My family had its own problems. Then an opportunity arose for Gustavo and me to live on our own. There was a custodial job in Miraflores. In exchange for keeping the building clean, we got an apartment on the roof. I lived in that apartment for eight months, acting like the ideal mother and wife, but I could not stand people's indifference. Everybody lived their own lives; no one spoke to anyone else. I just took care of my child and waited for my husband's return. I remember feeling that, on the one hand, I was happy with my family, but, on the other, totally frustrated as a person. I missed Villa El Salvador, its gatherings, the neighbors, and the life of my people.

I return to Villa El Salvador.

One day a neighbor's clothes were stolen from the roof, and a lady shouted at me, suggesting it was my family who had stolen them during one of their visits. I became furious at the very idea. I shouted at her, expressing all of my frustration and all of my feelings about class discrimination. I couldn't take it any longer. We said our good-byes and returned to Villa El Salvador.

In 1983 I returned to my community. I again lived with my mother; there wasn't an alternative. I did it with the hope of helping out my husband, so we could get a house. I got a job in a private school and did some substitute-teaching work in Public School 6070. Later, David, our second and unexpected child, came. My husband gave me the strength to have the baby, and my mother and youngest sister helped to care for both of our children. I taught literacy classes in the evenings. We founded a mothers' club, Micaela Bastidas, hoping to prevent any manipulation of the mothers by institutions such as OFASA [Adventist Philanthropic Office for Social Action] and others. It was a good experience. I worked morning, afternoon, and night.

I was director of a mothers' club for three years.

Being director of a mothers' club helped me to understand women's problems. I became conscious of women's roles and of their marginalization. Even though they worked outside the home, because they were women, their household duties didn't diminish. I understood, too, just how macho my own husband was. There were constant fights because I wanted him to assume some of the household chores.

At the end of 1983, a group of women from the mothers' club wanted to clean the streets, as other women's groups had been doing. I agreed and helped them with some cleaning tasks. Previously, a group of them had come to my house to propose the formation of a women's federation within our own group so that some could donate food [to the communal kitchen] instead of participating in cleaning duties. They asked my advice. I said that I didn't understand the role of a women's federation if its only purpose was to acquire food. They said that Señora Erlinda asked them to form the women's club with the women who do the sweeping. I told them I didn't understand why a women's club was needed if we already had a mothers' club because only women could be mothers. I didn't perceive any difference, and it also seemed like a duplication of effort. If it was a question of getting food, we could change the name from mothers' club to women's club.

It was time for a women's conference in Villa El Salvador.

The señoras asked me, along with two other delegates, to represent them at the convention where the Women's Federation was formed. I attended with my son David. When we got to the movie theater Madrid, we met many women from other organizations, including those from mothers' clubs. They were all trying to be part of the conference. Erlinda decided who would enter. I knew her because she had participated in the occupation of Public School 6066. When she recognized me, she refused to allow me to participate as a delegate. The women from the cleaning group told her that I was their representative, and that she should let me enter. Juana Bendezú, who also had participated in the school occupations, convinced Erlinda that I should be allowed to enter. I thought about the role of various factions at that convention, even though I did not understand them very well. Queta headed up the minority faction and Erlinda, the majority. They asked me to serve as secretary. I did not understand this federation business because it seemed that the only women who were attending were those from the cleaning groups; the majority of the women in the other organizations did not participate.

I had a small child, and I did not have time to dedicate to any federation. I thought of the manipulation that probably had occurred during the time of the school occupations. I began to think that maybe I should take the job, so I could better work for the women from my mothers' club. I was elected as undersecretary of the organization, and a new stage began in my personal life and in terms of my growth as a director. I was named president during the second Women's Federation convention of 1986, and I was reelected in May 1988.

From María Elena's Notebook, January–February 1992.

Ayer tuve a la muerte cerca.
Al ver a la familia de Andrés Sosa,*
a sus hijos que se desgarraban de dolor,
de impotencia,
sentí la muerte cerca.
Más cerca que antes.

Comprendí que difícil es el sacrificio.
Pensé en mis hijos, mi vida y mi historia,
pero cerca a la muerte sentí el amor,
este amor que ahora siento por ti,
mis hijos y mi pueblo,
y volví a sentir la vida cerca de mí.

Pensé que pese al dolor profundo que pudiera dejar,
siento que ya viví lo mejor de mi vida.
De mi niñez recuerdo a mi madre trabajando,
a mis hermanos enérgicos en nuestra educación,
la tristeza de no tener a mi padre cerca.
Pero también cuando pisé por primera vez el desierto
empecé a vivir los mejores años de mi vida.
Aunque con mis hermanos nos íbamos al colegio sin comer,
estábamos felices.

*Miembro del Bloque Populario Revolucionario (BPR), agrupación
conformada por disidentes del prosoviético Partido Comunista Peruano.
Fue asesinado en Villa El Salvador el 24 de enero de 1992 presuntamente
por miembros del Movimiento Revolucionario Tupac Amaru (MRTA).
María Elena asistió a su funeral.

Recuerdo cuando iba a la iglesia y me hice catequista.
Recuerdo a "Los Hijos del Pueblo,"
al grupo "Renovación,"
a los niños de los grupos 12 y 18
sentados en los ladrillos y en los tablones que ponía Gustavo
para que pintaran.

Recuerdo las luchas para organizarnos y estudiar,
las faenas comunales y las escuelas populares.
A Ana, a los profesores del SUTEP,
las ollas comunales.

Las marchas interminables e incontables
y a las mujeres organizadas.
Nuestras alegrías, penas y logros alcanzados.
A mis niños del colegio Miguel Grau, el 6070.

Entonces sigo recordando
y siento que he vivido lo más hermoso de mi vida.
A mis hijos,
la ternura de David y la timidez de Gustavito.
Este amor tan infinito,
a mis hijos,
a mi pueblo que sufre y se corroe el alma.
Su alegría de las polladas y festivales deportivos.

Cómo vivo, Dios mío.
Gracias por darme ¡todo!
El amor,
el dar todo lo que pude
de mí misma.
Todo.

Gracias Dios mío por seguirme dando la vida.
Febrero de 1992

Yesterday death came near to me
when I saw the family of Andrés Sosa,*
his children rent by grief,
and impotence.
I felt death near,
nearer than before.

I understood how difficult sacrifice is.
I thought about my children, my life and my history.
But close to death, I felt love, too,
that love I now feel for you,
my children and my people,
and I felt life rise within me again.

In spite of the deep sorrow I might cause,
I had lived the best years of my life.
I remembered my mother, working when I was a child,
my lively brothers at school, the sadness of
not having my father near.
Yet, when I first stepped onto the desert,
the best years of my life began.
Even though we went to school hungry,
we were happy.

I remember when I went to church
and studied catechism.
I remember the "Children of the People,"
and the youth from Renovación,
the children from groups 12 and 18
seated on the bricks and boards that Gustavo brought
so they could paint.

I remember the struggle to organize and the struggle to study,
the communal tasks and the people's schools,
and Ana, and the professors from SUTEP,
the communal kettles.

*Member of the Popular Revolutionary Block, formed by dissidents of
the pro-Soviet Peruvian Communist Party. Sosa was assassinated in Villa
El Salvador on January 24, 1992, presumably by members of the Túpac
Amaru Revolutionary Movement (MRTA). María Elena attended his funeral.

I recall the interminable and innumerable marches
and the women—organized.
Our happiness, pain and accomplishments,
and my students in the Miguel Grau School, number 6070.

Then I continue to remember
and know I've already lived the most beautiful years of my life.
My children,
the tenderness of David and the shyness of Gustavito.
This infinite love
for my children,
for my people whose souls are consumed,
yet they are happy at the barbecues and sport celebrations.

My God, how I've lived.
Thank you for giving me so much!
Love,
the opportunity to give my all—
Everything.

Thank you my God for continuing to give me life.
February 1992

Afterword

One week after María Elena's death, Gina Vargas wrote a short testimonial to her friend. María Elena and Gina were of different circumstances — economic, age, race, and culture — but they had developed a strong friendship. Gina was the academically oriented feminist, the founder of the Flora Tristán Center for the Peruvian Woman. María Elena was from the popular class. She had never referred to herself as a feminist, yet many Peruvian women consider her to have been a formidable one. According to Vargas, María Elena's death was "foretold." She wrote that, intellectually, María Elena's friends knew she was in danger, but they were from "a world of living energy — personal and social — of the world of life, not that of terror and of death," and their living world dimmed their awareness of danger from the death world.[1] She described her friend as "a charismatic and consensual leader, who communicated decisiveness, power and joy — much joy."[2]

Some of their mutual friends viewed the relationship as a sign of the potential for union between the popular and feminist streams of the women's movement. Vargas agreed that the relationship they enjoyed bridged the gap, but noted that it meant much more than that: "We were peers. We built a relationship of admiration, love, friendship, necessity. It was this relationship which overcame the most paralyzing aspects of the differences that exist between women, and which released the wealth of our diversity."[3]

In 1984, Vargas had run for Parliament as an independent but was still on the roll of the United Left. The left provided very little support to women candidates at that time. María Elena, however, gave her friend outright support, and she asked nothing in return, despite her prominent role as president of the Popular Women's Federation of Villa El Salvador.

At the end of 1989, Vargas went to Holland to undertake work at The Hague. Before her departure, María Elena and the Women's Federation held a farewell party for her in Villa. Not wanting to risk the trip back to her apartment in Lima after having enjoyed herself at the party, Vargas spent the night in María Elena's house:

> They cooked for me, we danced, we drank beer. When, at eleven o'clock, the last bottle was empty, I went with María Elena and Esperanza, another leader of FEPOMUVES [the Women's Federation], to find a liquor store open at that time of night. Everything was closed but we nonetheless managed to get one of them to open up, without realizing that the dogs were loose. The result was that one of them bit Esperanza rather badly and we ended up in the hospital at around four in the morning. Esperanza, a strong woman, was badly scared and I, also a strong woman, was even more so. On the way to the hospital Esperanza was weeping and crying that she was going to die; I could hardly drive because of the tears streaming from my eyes. María Elena—with her capacity for leadership in the best and worst conditions, in battles both large and small—first comforted us and then shouted: how is it possible for two grown-up feminist leaders to die because of a dog bite and a little blood? (She employed, of course, stronger language than I am using here.) We got back to Villa at around 4:30 in the morning. The women had already left the party, furious because they thought we had gone off to get drunk on our own.[4]

María Elena later wanted to organize another farewell to be held at Vargas's own home. Vargas insisted that María Elena come with her bodyguards, remembering that, in the planning, María Elena had told Vargas that the farewell (held three weeks before her death) would have to be a very special event since she might not be around when her friend returned.

* * *

Sendero continued its siege against women activists by killing three women shortly after María Elena's murder: Marina Oroña Barbarán was a Vaso de Leche committee president from the district of Junín; Verónica Pérez de Mantari was president of a neighbor's group in Huancayo; and

Rebeca Fernández Cartagena was secretary-general of a *pueblo joven* in Lima called Villa Solidaridad.[5]

Violence directed against women by Sendero Luminoso has subsided in recent years, but the social and economic conditions that gave rise to it, as well as to the December 17, 1996, taking of over three hundred hostages at the Japanese ambassador's residence in Lima by members of the Tupac Amaru Revolutionary Movement (MRTA), remain the same. It may be too early to predict if President Fujimori's rescue of the remaining seventy-two hostages on April 22, 1997, will quell future terrorist activities. And although most Peruvians praised Fujimori for his audacious act, many Peruvian women activists decried the deaths of all fourteen rebels, including two teenaged girls. None was taken prisoner, despite Fujimori's promise to use force only if the hostages were harmed.[6]

The Peruvian military does not inspire trust. After all, President Fujimori used it to shut down Congress when he assumed emergency powers in 1992, and, according to Amnesty International, the military remains under suspicion for past egregious human rights abuses.[7]

And people are becoming disenchanted with Fujimori. There is still hunger, recession, and widespread unemployment. Will he run for a third term? He and his supporters claim he's entitled, given that his first term began before the implementation of the new constitution.[8]

In the meantime, it is the women who continue to improve conditions of daily life. In an August 29, 1999, article in the *New York Times,* Clifford Krauss described their efforts: in the mountain village of Nuñhuaycco, a children's playground, built next to the tombs of forty villagers, victims of Sendero violence; communal gardens; mothers' clubs sponsoring banks that make small business loans to women; government clinics that counsel women on family planning; women serving on municipal councils; the democratization of municipal governments.[9]

Women are bringing a new perspective to the decision-making process. Long deprived of women's wisdom in the public domain, Peru will be the better for it. It is for this that María Elena Moyano died. She brought wisdom and courage to the Peruvian crucible of poverty and violence. A woman of color, she understood the universality of the movement in which she played a dramatic role. Shortly before her death, María Elena described her vision of a social revolution in Peru, which included the achievement of democratic relationships between men and women and an end to social and cultural hierarchies based on gender. She fought for her country as fiercely as any military leader, she fought for women as steadfastly as a suffragist, and she fought for mothers as unremittingly as any mother who will feed, clothe, and shelter her children, despite overwhelming obstacles.

María Elena is a towering heroine for women—regardless of their marital status, economic class, race, and culture—and especially for ordinary women who do battle every day to bring about social justice in their own communities.

Notes

Women in Peru: A History of Struggle and Courage

1. Gina Vargas, *500 años de patriarcado en el nuevo mundo* (Santo Domingo, Dominican Republic: Red Entre Mujeres, Centro de Investigación para la Acción Feminina [CIPAF], 1992), 140.

2. Ibid., 143.

3. Ibid., 143–45.

4. Magda Portal, *El aprismo y la mujer* (Lima: Editorial Cooperativa Aprista "Atahualpa," 1933), 56, quoted in Francesca Miller, *Latin American Women and the Search for Social Justice* (Hanover, N.H.: University Press of New England, 1991), 101.

5. Portal, 17, quoted in Miller, 102.

6. Miller, 102.

7. Magda Portal, "¿Quienes traicionaron al pueblo?" *Cuadernos de divulgación popular* 1 (April 1950): 12, quoted in Miller, 121.

8. Portal, ibid., 7–8, quoted in Miller, 121.

9. Miller, 121.

10. Magda Portal, "Yo soy Magda Portal," in *Ser mujer en el Perú*, 2d ed., interviews by Esther Andradi and Ana María Portugal (Lima: Takapu Editores, 1979), 209–30, quoted in Miller, 121.

11. James Brown Scott, *The International Conferences of American States, 1889–1928* (New York: Oxford University Press, 1931), vii, quoted in Miller, 95.

12. Miller, 110–11.

13. Mary Cannon, "Women's Organizations in Ecuador, Paraguay, and Peru," *Bulletin of the Pan-American Union* 77 (November 1943): 604, quoted in Miller, 115.

14. Ibid.

15. Miller, 143.

16. Sonia Montecino, "La conquista de las mujeres: Las cautivas, simbólica de lo femenino en América Latina," in Vargas, *500 años*, 67–71.

17. Virginia Vargas, *El aporte de la rebeldía de las mujeres* (Lima: Centro de la Mujer Peruana, Flora Tristán, Parque Hernán Velarde 42, 1989), 34.

18. Miller, 203.

19. Maruja Barrig, "The Difficult Equilibrium between Bread and Roses: Women's Organizations and Democracy in Peru," in *The Women's Movement in Latin America*, ed. Jane S. Jaquette (Boulder Colo.: Westview Press, 1994), 159.

20. Elizabeth Jelin, *About Women, about Human Rights* (Lima: Red Entre Mujeres Diálogo Sur-Norte, Parque Hernán Velarde 42, 1993), 45.

21. Ibid., 39.

22. Virginia Guzmán, *Los azarosos años 80 aciertos y desencuentros del movimiento de mujeres en Latinoamérica y el Caribe* (Lima: Red Entre Mujeres Diálogo Sur-Norte, 1994), 17–18.

23. James Brooke, "Peru: On the Very Fast Track," *Wall Street Journal,* January 31, 1995, C1.

24. Hannah Arendt, *The Origins of Totalitarianism* (New York: Harcourt, Brace and World, 1973), and Claude Lefort, "Los derechos del hombre y el estado benefactor," *Vuelta* (Mexico), July 1987, quoted in Jelin, *About Women,* 15.

25. Guzmán, *Los azarosos años 80,* 28.

26. Marta Lamas, "El movimiento feminista Méjicano y su papel en la formulación de las pólíticas públicas," quoted ibid., 34.

27. Carlos Iván Degregori, "Origins and Logic of Shining Path: Two Views," in *Shining Path of Peru,* ed. David Scott Palmer (New York: St. Martin's Press, 1992), 37.

28. Quoted ibid.

29. Robin Kirk, *Untold Terror: Violence against Women in Peru's Armed Conflict* (New York: Americas Watch and the Women's Rights Project, 1992), 2.

30. Ibid., 4.

31. Ibid., 18.

32. Ibid., 17.

33. Interview with Luis Arce Borja, *Der Spegel* (Germany), July 1992, quoted ibid., 5.

34. Thomas Kamm, "Peru Strives to Turn Its Fortunes around with Terrorist's Arrest," *Wall Street Journal,* February 25, 1992, A8.

35. Efraín Gonzales de Olarte, "Peruvian Aftershocks: The Faultlines of Governance," *North-South Focus* 2, no. 4 (North-South Center, University of Miami, 1993), 1.

36. Matt Moffett, "Fujimori Has Tamed Terrorism and Inflation but Means Still Rankle," *Wall Street Journal,* February 22, 1994, A6.

37. Guzmán, *Los azaroso años 80,* 24.

38. Susan Cochrane, *Fertility and Education: What Do We Really Know?* (Baltimore: Johns Hopkins University Press, 1979; B. Wolfe and J. Behram, "Who Is Schooled in Developing Countries? The Role of Income, Parental Schooling, Sex, Residence and Family Size," *Economics of Education Review* 3, no. 3 (1985): 231–45, in *Una Nueva Lectura: Género en el Desarrollo,* ed. Virginia Guzmán, Patricia Portocarrero, and Virginia Vargas (Lima: Red entre Mujeres, Ediciones Flira Tristán, Parque Hernán Velarde #42, 1991), 195.

39. Patricia Ruiz Bravo, "Imposición o autonomía sobre la relación entre ONG's y agéncias de cooperación a propósito de la perspectiva de género," *Propuestas,* vol. 1 (Lima, Peru: Entre Mujeres Diálogo Sur-Norte, 1994), 8.

40. Andy Wehkamp, Introduction, in *Engendering Development Experiences in Gender and Development Planning,* ed. Maruja Barrig and Andy Wehkamp (The Hague, Netherlands: NOVIB, Amaliastraat 7, 2514JC, 1994), 10.

41. UNIFEM, "Gender Relations and Institutional Development: Dilemmas and Challenges Facing NGOs in Latin America," *UNIFEM Fact Sheet* (New York: United Nations, 1993), 1.

42. Kathleen Nilan, "Flora Tristan," in *Encyclopedia of 1848 Revolutions,* ed. James Chastain (1999); Miller, *Latin American Women,* 14.

43. Centro de la Mujer Peruana Flora Tristán, *Primer borrador de discusión sobre los objetivos de Flora Tristán* (Lima, 1993), 4.

44. Centro de la Mujer Peruana Flora Tristán, *Perfil Institucional* (Lima 1998), 1–2.

45. Vargas, *El aporte,* 127.

46. Ibid., 134.

47. Ibid.

48. Ibid., 47–48.

49. Jelin, *About Women,* 135.

50. Vargas, *El aporte,* 42.

51. Ibid., 96–97.

52. Ibid., 25–27.

53. Ibid., 105–12, 130.

María Elena Moyano: The Life and Death of a Peruvian Activist

1. "Madres no se doblegan," *La República* (Lima), December 11, 1991, quoted in Kirk, *Untold Terror,* 53.

2. Ibid.

3. *La República,* February 6, 1992, cited ibid., 54.

Part One

1. María Elena refers to the 1990 presidential election of engineer Alberto Fujimori.

2. This song of the women of Villa El Salvador is a waltz from the Song Workshop of the People's Communication Center, Villa El Salvador.

3. In 1985 Pope John Paul II visited Villa El Salvador because of its large concentration of faithful.

4. Villa El Salvador was founded in 1973. In 1987 it received the Spanish Prince of Asturias Award and was proclaimed "Messenger City of Peace." In January 1993 it was named "Messenger City of Peace and Development" during the visit of Javier Pérez de Cuellar, then secretary-general of the United Nations.

5. The members of the Sendero Luminoso (Shining Path), the Peruvian Communist Party, are known as Senderistas.

6. The organizing commission that gave rise to the federation was installed in 1980.

7. The first convention of the Popular Women's Federation of Villa El Salvador met in the Madrid movie theater in December 1983.

8. At this writing, the federation was preparing for its fifth convention, when a new directorate was to be elected. María Elena was in charge of program evaluation when she was assassinated, having earlier served as president for two terms.

9. The winner in Lima's municipal elections of November 1983 was the United Left electoral alliance. The Vaso de Leche committees formed part of the Emergency Plan for Nutrition and Health that was designed in 1984 by the Lima city government.

10. Law 24059, which gave support to the Vaso de Leche program, was promulgated on January 6, 1985.

11. In October 1986 the first Metropolitan Coordinating Committee for Vaso de Leche was elected, with thirty-three representatives from each of Lima's districts. The second metropolitan convention took place on October 26 and 28, 1990.

12. The Third Assembly of Vaso de Leche districts took place on October 30–31, 1992. There were 400 delegates from 13 centers that represented 107,000 beneficiaries, among them children and the elderly. The women advanced their organization, regulating the milk distribution process, and unanimously agreed to name their event after María Elena Moyano, at a time when the Fujimori government was cutting the Vaso de Leche budget from 507.3 to 289.7 million soles.

13. Even though there has been no census, it is estimated that there are approximately 6,000 communal kitchens in the Lima metropolitan area today.

14. The federation kitchens began to operate in Villa in September 1984. Since 1980, however, some of them had been linked to certain government agencies, political parties, and other institutions.

15. In 1992 the government had no real social assistance program for women's organizations.

16. Care Peru is a nongovernmental social assistance agency.

17. The Program for Direct Assistance was created during the term of President Alán García Pérez (1985–90).

18. The people of Villa El Salvador relied on the municipal government of Villa María del Triunfo until 1983, when Villa El Salvador acquired its autonomy.

19. María Elena refers to the 1989 municipal elections.

20. In 1989 María Elena Moyano, candidate of the United Left, was elected deputy mayor of the municipality of Villa El Salvador.

21. PAIT was created during the presidential term of Alán García Pérez to alleviate acute unemployment in the country.

22. These commissions included representatives from the state Ministry of Health, local government, and community organizations.

23. In 1991 an epidemic of cholera afflicted 220,000 persons in Peru, causing the death of 2,100 the first year.

24. María Elena Moyano created the municipal monitor project. It no longer receives municipal support.

25. This is the newspaper of the Shining Path that circulated in Peru until April 1992.

26. Since 1988, the Women's Federation has had a center that houses a medical clinic and a library.

27. Enrique Castilla was a union leader in the company Textiles La Unión and a member of the Central Committee of the Mariátegui United Party. He was assassinated in October 1990.

28. On September 9, 1991, Sendero dynamited a federation's center that supplied ninety communal kitchens.

29. From its 1984 founding until December 1988, María Elena belonged to the United Mariátegui Party. In 1992 she joined the Movement toward Socialism (MAS).

30. According to 1991 figures from the Human Rights Commission of the United Nations and Amnesty International, Peru was one of the countries with the greatest number of detained and disappeared in the world.

31. Javier Diez Canseco was national director of the United Mariátegui Party and a senator of the republic. Manuel Dammert was director of the Revolutionary Communist Party and a representative of the republic.

32. Open letter from María Elena Moyano, published by various media during September 1991, in response to accusations by Sendero Luminoso. The translation is literal.

33. MCB is a front organization of Sendero Luminoso that operated in the barrios of Lima.

34. Change 90 was the party that carried engineer Alberto Fujimori to the presidency in the 1990 elections.

35. Ernesto Castillo Páez, a sociology student at the Catholic University, disappeared after being detained by a police patrolman in Villa El Salvador on October 27, 1990.

36. At the close of the legislative session, on December 15, 1990, the Parliament approved Law 25307, the Assistance Act for the Nutrition Work of the Base Social Organizations. It was promulgated in February 1991. The executive had to approve the law and the accompanying budget. The National Commission of Communal Kitchens spearheaded the project.

37. Letter sent to Emma Hilario, director of the National Commission of Communal Kitchens, who had to go into exile after surviving an assassination attempt by Sendero on December 30, 1991. She was shot at while in her home in the *pueblo joven* Pamplona Alta.

38. On September 26, 1991, there was a mass demonstration and march from the Campo de Marte playing field to the Plaza San Martín. Its theme was "Against Hunger and Terror." The women's groups organized the event, which was the first mass demonstration during this period.

39. The National Popular Assembly (ANP) was an effort to centralize the people's organizations. It was created in 1987 but no longer exists.

40. Juana López León, the forty-seven-year-old general coordinator of Vaso de Leche for the John Paul II Center of Callao, was assassinated by Sendero Luminoso near her home at 6:30 A.M. on August 31, 1991.

Part Two

1. María Elena refers to the youth group Renovación. She was its president from 1973 to 1975.

2. José Rodríguez, former mayor of the district of Villa El Salvador.

3. In 1976 María Elena was chosen to be the first promoter of preschool education in a nonformal, experimental program called PRONOEI.

4. *Apros* refers to the militant members of the American Popular Revolutionary Alliance (APRA), one of the oldest political organizations in the history of the Peruvian Republic.

5. María Elena married Gustavo Pineki on March 28, 1980.

Afterword

1. Gina Vargas, "My Friend María Elena" (The Hague, Netherlands, February 18, 1992), 1.

2. Ibid.

3. Ibid.

4. Ibid., 2.

5. Kirk, *Untold Terror*, 56.

6. Joshua Hammer, "Liberated," *Newsweek*, May 5, 1997, 36–39, and Art Babych, "Interchurch Group Call for Inquiry into Peru Hostage Rescue Deaths," *Florida Catholic*, May 1, 1997, A7.

7. "Riding a Tiger: Former General Blows the Whistle on Army Violations in Peru," *Amnesty Action* (Spring 1997), 3.

8. Clifford Krauss, "Fujimori's Burden in Peru," *New York Times on the Web*, January 14, 1999.

9. Clifford Krauss, "A Revolution Peru's Rebels Didn't Intend," *New York Times on the Web*, August 29, 1999.

Selected Bibliography

Prepared by Elizabeth Toguchi Kayo

Interviews with and Presentations by María Elena Moyano Delgado

1988   "Movimiento de mujeres populares." In *Diez ensayos y una historia colectiva*, 275–309. Lima: Centro de la Mujer Peruana Flora Tristán.

1990a   "María Elena, flor de cactus." In Sonia Goldenberg, *Reportaje al Perú anónimo*, 2d ed., 141–46. Lima: Francisco Campodónico.

1990b   "María Elena Moyano." In Margarita Giesecke, Carmen Checa, and Alberto Giesecke, *Violencia estructural en el Perú: historias de vida*, 61–69. Lima: APEP.

1990c   "Conquistando un espacio." *La Tortuga* (Lima) 36: 14–19. Interview with Armida Testino.

1990d   "¿Dirigimos o cocinamos el Vaso de Leche?" *Pagina Libre* (Lima), August 12, B2–B7.

1991a   "La fuerza feminina ante las luchas populares." *Tierra Nuestra* (Mexico City) 4: 43–46. Interview with María Flores Estrada.

1991b   "Participación de la mujer en los gobiernos locales." Paper presented at the international forum of the same name. Quito, Ecuador: Flora Tristán archives.

1991c   "Sendero será derrotado." Domingo. *La República* (Lima), September 22. Interview with Mariella Balbi.

1992a   "Carta abierta: Yo construyo, jamás destruyo . . ." *La República* (Lima), February 17, 3.

1992b   "Contra el hambre y el terror." *Ideéle* (IDL) 4, no. 35 (March): 4–5.

1992c   "Malena madre." Domingo. *La República* (Lima), February 23. Interview with Luis Alberto Chávez.

1992d   "María Elena: Vida y libertad." *Socialismo y Participación* (Lima) 57 (March): 1–8. Interview with Sonia Luz Carillo.

1992e   "Nada podrá detener la revolución doméstica." *La República* (Lima), February 18. Interview with Agencia Internacional EFE.

1992f   "Organización popular es la alternativa al terror." *El Peruano* (Lima), February 17, A5. Interview with María Flores Estrada. Reprinted in *Tierra Nuestra* (Mexico City), October 1991.

1992g   "Ser dirigente, mujer y autoridad." In *Mujer y liderazgo: entre la familia y la política*, edited by Patricia Córdova. Lima: Asociación Civil Estudios y Publicaciones Urbanas (YUNTA).

About María Elena Moyano Delgado

"El asesinato de María Elena Moyano: El gran error de Guzmán." *La República* (Lima), February 20, 1992, 17.

Azcueta, Michel. "María Elena: La luz contra las tinieblas." *La República* (Lima), February 17, 1992, 7.

Azofra, Félix. "María Elena Moyano." *Enfoques de mujer* (GEMPA) (Paraguay) 7, no. 22 (March 1992): 32–33.

Blondet, Cecilia. *Las mujeres y el poder: Una historia de Villa El Salvador.* Urbanización, migraciones, y cambios en la sociedad Peruana no. 10. Lima: Instituto de Estudios Peruanos (IEP), 1991.

Bonnet, Nicole. "María Helena Moyano, adjointe au maire d'un bidonville de Lima, a été assaissinée par le sentier lumineaux." *Le Monde* (Paris), February 18, 1992.

———. "Contra el pueblo y contra las mujeres." *Mujer/Fempress* (Santiago, Chile), April 1992, 1–2.

———. "Mujeres amenazadas." *Mujer/Fempress* (Santiago, Chile), October 1992, 4.

Centro de Documentación sobre la Mujer (CENDOC-MUJER). "El moviemiento popular de mujeres como respuesta a la crisis." Paquete informativo, 2. Lima: CENDOC-MUJER, 1992.

Chávez, Luis Alberto. "La autodefensa del Salvador." *La República* (Lima), February 23, 1992, 4–7.

Coll, Pilar. "El pueblo construye, sendero destruye." *Carta Circular* (CNDDHH) (Lima), March 1992, 2.

Correa de Belaúnde, Violeta. "Biografía no vivida." *La Tortuga* 45 (1992): 13.

D'Ornellas, Manuel. "Esa muerte anunciada." *Expreso* (Lima), February 18, 1992, A2.

Escajadillo, C., Luis. "María Elena Moyano: La mató el narcotráfico." *La República* (Lima), February 21, 1992, 17.

Gorriti, Gustavo. "El leviatán y la heroína." *Caretas* (Lima), March 2, 1992, 25, 87.

Guzmán, Virginia. "Perú: La fuerza puede estar en las mujeres." *Mujeres en acción* (ISIS Internacional) (Santiago, Chile) 2 (1992): 16–22.

Hernández, Zoila. "Hacía la autonomía total." *Mujer y sociedad* (Lima) 13 (1987): 5–6.

"Hora de unirse y organizarse." *Expreso* (Lima), February 18, 1992, A18.

Lauer, Mirko. "A dinamita, sendero estrecha el cerco." *Cambio* (Madrid, Spain), March 2, 1992, 16–17.

"Por María Elena, por nuestro pueblo: ¿Será posible unirnos? se lo debemos." *Signos* (Lima) 12, no. 15 (February 28, 1992). (Special issue dedicated to María Elena Moyano.)

"María Elena Moyano: Coraje y mucho más." *Páginas* (CEP) (Lima) 17, nos.

114–15 (April–June 1992): 7–17. (Special issue dedicated to María Elena Moyano.)

"María Elena Moyano, mártir del pueblo." *Ideéle* (IDL) 4, no. 35 (March 1992): 3–11. (Special issue dedicated to María Elena Moyano.)

Massa, Alberto. "Sueños de una noche de verano." *Oiga* (Lima), March 23, 1992, 27.

Miloslavich Tupac, Diana. "Con la honda de David." Domingo. *La República* (Lima), March 8, 1992, 32.

Miro Quesada G., Luis. "Homenaje a María Elena Moyano." *El Comercio* (Lima), February 24, 1992.

Montoya, Rodrigo. "Desde otra orilla: Homenaje a María Elena Moyano." *La República* (Lima), February 26, 1992.

Monzu, Alegría. "Yo fui su amiga." *Cambio* (Madrid, Spain), March 2, 1992, 17.

"La muerte anunciada." *Caretas*, February 17, 1992, 26–32, 93.

Mujica, Rosa María. "Si cae Villa . . . ¿Quién será el siguiente?" *La República* (Lima), February 21, 1992, 16.

Mujica Álvarez Calderón, María. "¿Perú, qué has hecho de tu hermana?" *El Comercio*, March 3, 1992, A2.

Munive, Mario. "¡No nos moverán!" *La República* (Lima), September 10, 1989, 20–22.

Orbegozo, Manuel Jesús. "María Elena Moyano: ¡Presente!" *El Comercio*, February 23, 1992. (Sunday supplement.)

Pisano, Margarita. "Ni sacrificios ni héroes, sólo buena humanidad." *La Nación* (Santiago, Chile), March 17, 1992.

Prado, Jorge del. "María Elena Moyano: Convicción, consecuencia y coraje." *La República* (Lima), February 24, 1992.

Ricketts Rey de Castro, Patricio. "Las víctimas del terror." *Expreso* (Lima), February 19, 1992, A19.

Ruiz Eldredge, Alberto. "La acción del hogar contra el mal: Micaela, María, María Elena." *La República* (Lima), February 27, 1992.

Schele de García, Carmen; Favre, Julio. "Un símbolo de coraje." *La Tortuga* (Lima) 45 (1992): 32.

Silvestre, Miguel. "Vida y muerte en Villa El Salvador." *Sí* (Lima), February 24, 1992, 24–28.

Tello, María del Pilar. "María Elena: Una heroína civil." *Gestión* (Lima), February 18, 1992.

———. "El asesinato de María Elena Moyano: El gran error de Guzman." *La Republica* (Lima), February 20, 1992, 17.

Tudela, Chopitea, Alejandro. "Malena eterna." Suplemento dominical. *El Comercio* (Lima), February 23, 1992. (Sunday supplement.)

Tuesta Soldevilla, Fernando. "Villa El Salvador: Los caminos alternativos de la democracia." Manuscript, Lima, Peru, 1992.

Vargas, Gina. "El asesinato de la madre coraje." *La Nación* (Santiago, Chile), March 8, 1992. (Extract of an article that appeared in *La República de las mujeres* [Montevideo, Uruguay, 1992] under the title "Crónica de una muerte anunciada.")

———. "Carta por María Elena Moyano." *La Carta* (CEAAL) (Santiago, Chile), March–April 1992, 3.

Villarán, Susana. "María Elena: ¿Te diste cuenta quién te mató?" *La República* (Lima), February 27, 1992.

Videos

Asociación de Comunicadores Sociales. *Calandria.* 1992. (Documentary about the life of María Elena Moyano.)

Lucar, Nicolás. Television interview with María Elena Moyano. *La Revista dominical.* Channel 4, Lima, September 1992.

Luna, Lola. Interview with María Elena Moyano. Grupo Warmi. Spain. 1986.

Video material from the cultural calendars of Channels 2 and 7, Lima.

Radio

Programing from *Nuestra Vida.*

Index

Diana Miloslavich Tupac studied literature at the National University of San Marcos in Lima. She went to Mexico to participate in a study on ethnic minorities and human rights, and there she became a member of the Mexican Solidarity Committee for Guatemalan refugees. Upon her return to Peru, she rejoined the women's movement.

Patricia S. Taylor Edmisten is an independent scholar and retired professor of the sociological foundations of education at the University of West Florida. She has worked in Peru as a Peace Corps volunteer and as a consultant for the United Nations.

CPSIA information can be obtained
at www.ICGtesting.com
Printed in the USA
FSOW02n0944181214
3964FS